HAMMERED

MEMOIR OF AN ADDICT

HAMMERED
MEMOIR OF AN ADDICT

GEOFF BROWN

Asylum Books

HAMMERED: MEMOIR OF AN ADDICT
Geoff Brown

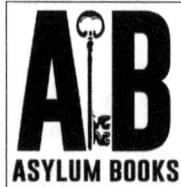

Asylum Books
An imprint of Cohesion Press
Mayday Hills Lunatic Asylum
Beechworth, Australia

ACKNOWLEDGEMENTS

For Dawn: You're always there for me. I couldn't have finished this without you, and my life with you is better than I could ever have imagined.

Thanks and much love to David, Leah, Mike and Molly, Charley, Naomi, and Julian for all the love and support, AJ, Matt, Dean, Steve Mc, Mandy, and all my other new friends in our new life, to Kris Saknussemm for writing the introduction so beautifully, and, of course, the Legumeman Books guys and gals (Matt, Rob and Brooke) for believing in this story enough to publish the first edition.

You all helped in many ways.

And last, but never least, for Mum and Dad. Thank you for loving me, no matter what.

Heroin is an illegal opioid that slows the brain and central nervous system functions. It's commonly known as 'smack', 'slow', 'H' or 'hammer'.

The state of being stoned on heroin is commony called 'on the nod' due to the look of being half asleep or partially unconscious.

CONTENTS

INTRODUCTION

This is a painfully sharp account of a life that turned around. It avoids the clichés of memoirs of addiction that are 'inspiring' and 'redemptive', although it is that finally, in spades. Along the way though, and what I admire about it most, is that it's gutter truthful about the simple, brutal waste of innocence that drug dependence is — on the hour. Most importantly, and what moves this story into a higher register and the realm of larger social concern, is it's recognition of the insidious nature of self-denial, which is the most dangerous and widespread drug there will ever be. Neil Young laid it down, "A little part of it in everyone."

Because of the nature of the drug life involved, many people will find connections with the writing of people like William Burroughs, but I actually see an older linkage to the work of Malcolm Lowry, who wrote so poignantly of alcoholism, lost hope and hope regained.

Geoff Brown is a writer who stays out of both his own shadow and light, and lets you decide which best suits. The message is that this all could happen to you, or to someone you know and love. It's actually remarkably easy to go down slow — because that's the way it happens. Maybe we all can survive our wrong turns.

I'd add that we are given here a finely edged portrait of a special and complex part of the city of Melbourne, which is well worth reading in its own right. As Sly Stone, one of my countrymen who has had more than a little trouble with drugs would say: "You can't get to it if you haven't been through it."

This is a hard journey well-shared and a book that risks real sadness to tell its human truth.

-Kris Saknussemm, author

1

PREFACE

This is a memoir of my well-over-twenty years of drug use.

I remember a lot of the events throughout these years. Some things just stick with me no matter how young or 'out of it' I was at the time. Usually the bad things, but sometimes the good. To say that my recollection of other events that add to these vivid memories to make up the total of this work can be hazy at times is certainly an understatement, which is why this is a memoir rather than autobiographical. For the timeline of my main substance-abusing years, I worked firstly from a police check listing all my arrests and court appearances, as well as the years I moved areas and went into rent agreements and worked for specific employers. From this, I filled in the blanks in between with the best memories I have, both good and bad. My internal dialogues, and most of the conversational episodes between myself and others, were formed using my recollection of myself, my perception of my mostly-unchanged personality, and how I believe I acted at the time of the event.

Recollections of others and their personalities and actions are due to my own impressions of them, as well as remembered events that outlined how I perceived them to be. I can only work from that. I changed a lot of names in the original release, and some have now been changed back to true first-name use.

I have also done my best to present an unbiased version of my actions, no matter the temptation to make myself seem better than I actually was.

I owe this work the bare truth, if it is to have any meaning in my ongoing journey or any ability to help others understand their own journey, or that of a loved one.

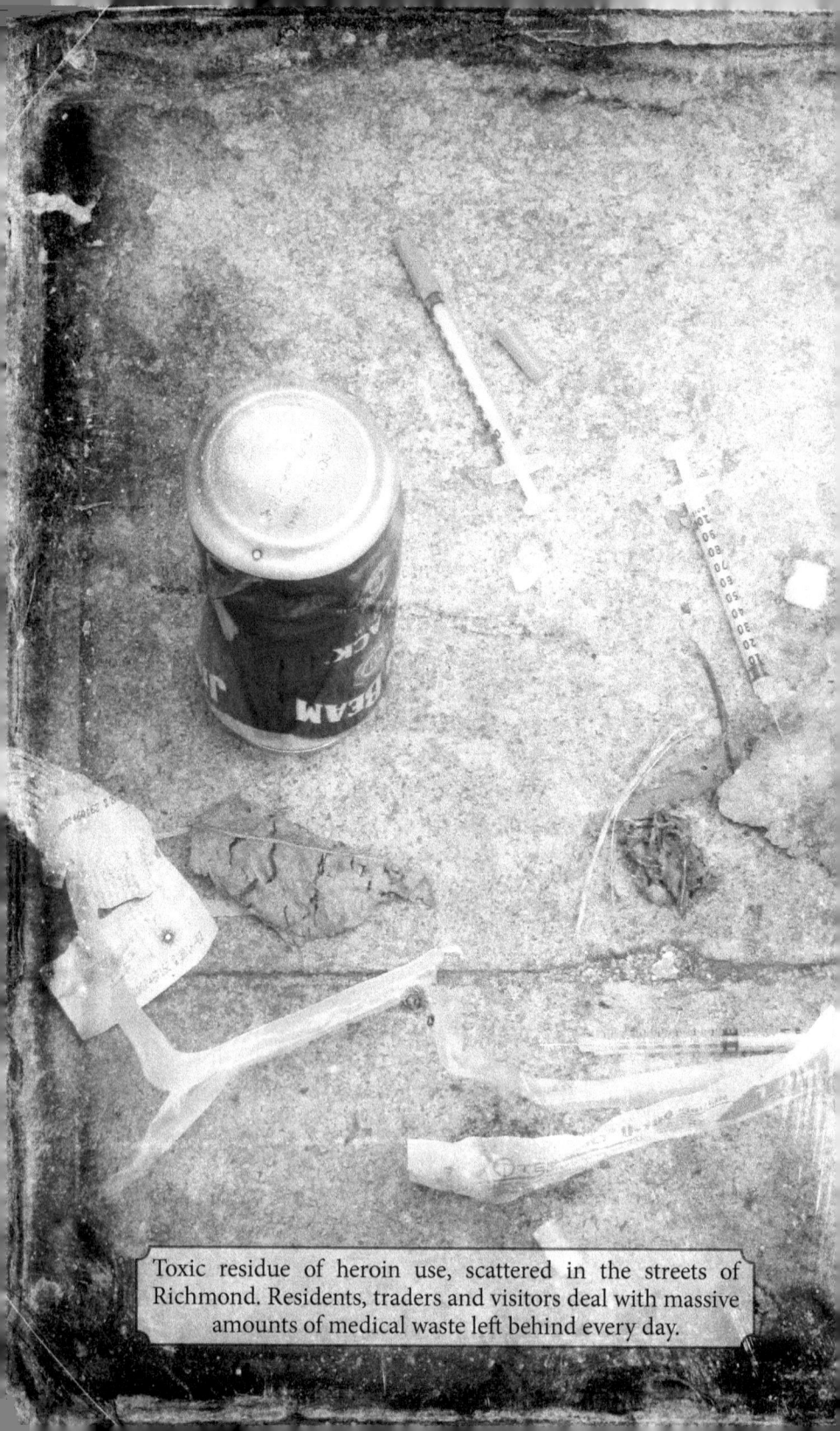

Toxic residue of heroin use, scattered in the streets of Richmond. Residents, traders and visitors deal with massive amounts of medical waste left behind every day.

SEPTEMBER 2005

Richmond, Melbourne

The setting seemed appropriate for where my life was at the moment.

The floor was wet with God knows what, and it stank like a cesspool. Scrawled graffiti, reminiscent of hieroglyphics, lined the dirty, peeling walls. Webs spun by spiders long dead hung thick in the corners. Cigarette butts, plastic spoons, used syringes and their plastic wrappers littered the rough concrete floor, punctuated now and then by broken glass or a crushed cigarette packet.

A pair of legs stuck out from one of the cubicles, feet splayed apart as though in death, one jeans leg soaking up an unidentified puddle from the floor, the denim already wet halfway to the knee. Their owner wasn't deceased, though, just asleep... the deep, dark sleep heroin gives you. I'd checked when I came in. We didn't want to be involved in anything official if someone else happened to enter the public toilet and found us shooting up next to a corpse.

I looked over at Carolyn, stoned out of her mind, and wondered just where we were going. Life was shit, and not getting any better. We were both unemployed and both heroin addicts. Even though I was a trained nurse, I hadn't worked in years, too busy looking for easy money and the next score.

Here we were, off our heads on heroin – again – sitting near the vomit of the dealer we'd scored from. He'd swallowed his gear, which was sealed in water balloons for just that situation, when an undercover cop grabbed him off the street in Richmond. After being released from the police station without charge due to lack of evidence, he had gone straight to the public toilets around the corner from the cop-shop – which is where I saw him – and drank a heap of water laced with salt from his backpack to make it easy to vomit it all back up.

I followed him into the toilet-block because I knew him from the street. The name he used with customers was Johnny. He usually had good stuff and his sizes were better than normal for street gear. Just as I walked into the toilet block, he threw up everywhere. The ballooned packages stood out in the stinking pool of vomit.

I bought two bile-covered deals from him with our last seventy dollars and, as he left, called Carolyn in for our hit of smack. At the time, I thought I was doing the right thing, but now I see the strange logic of giving poison to the one I loved.

Smack was our way of life. We lived to score, and scored to live.

I mulled up the hammer in a spoon and we had our taste. As I packed up our injecting gear, capping the syringes after rinsing them out, I wondered why other junkies felt the need to leave their used works lying around uncapped for someone to stick themselves with. It only took a second to pick everything up, and junkies lived with enough guilt as it was without adding more.

I felt all warm and fuzzy, relaxed for the first time that day. Usually, I had maybe an hour to enjoy it before I had to start thinking about getting some cash for the next score, but it was late and payday was tomorrow.

I had a pretty good system going. I would steal books from the bigger department stores and sell them to second-hand bookshops in the Eastern suburbs. The owners asked no questions and were always willing to take as many as I could get. In two hours I could steal enough to get a couple of hundred bucks, enough for a half-gram of gear

At this point, I had no real habit driving me, so I could afford to relax and enjoy the stone. We were in the women's toilets, where there were more stalls to hit up in. We'd tried to go to the disabled stall, with its own tap and more privacy, but some other junkie must have beaten us there. They were everywhere these days.

I looked up as a young girl, no more than fifteen or sixteen but an addict from the look of her, pushed through the door from the outside and went into one of the cubicles without giving us a second glance. Day-to-day life addiction is never easy.

💉 💉 💉

The best place for scoring drugs used to be St Kilda, but these days it was Richmond or Footscray. They took over as the heroin centres of Melbourne, and we knew Richmond so that was where we went to get the best deals on the best gear.

I looked over at the woman who used to be the love of my life sitting half-awake in that toilet in Richmond, and for the millionth time wished that things were different.

I finished packing our kit and went to rouse Carolyn so we could go sit in the park and just kick back and zone out for a while.

"C'mon, darl. Let's get out of this shithole," I said, unsure of whether I meant the toilet, the suburb, or the lifestyle.

"Yeah, righto. Y'wanna sit in the car for a bit before we go?"

"We could sit in the park," I suggested. "It's a beautiful day.

"Sounds like a plan," she replied.

In the old days, I'd need to find a way to earn some cash within an hour or two, one that wouldn't mess with my conscience too much. No bag snatches for me, no mugging of old ladies to get their pension cheques. I stole from the bigger stores, not from someone who worked forty hours a week to put food on the family table. Even an addict had to have *some* morals, however skewed they were.

A moral junkie. Is that an oxymoron?

I sometimes felt that I was so far off course that my moral compass was turning in circles.

Throughout my addiction, I hurt a lot of people; most often the ones who were closest to me. That was the life of an addict. It was easier to touch someone who cared for a few dollars, giving them a sob story that was far from the truth, than it was to hit up strangers.

Lying together on the grass, stoned and staring up at the clouds churning across the sky, it all seemed so distant. I was numb from the struggle. I didn't have the will to go on like this anymore. This wasn't living; this was just getting by day-to-day. There had to be a way out of this. I had to quit. I had to stop using hammer completely.

I'd tried to quit before, and each time I'd fucked up within days; sometimes within hours or even minutes of getting out of detox. Looking up at the sky, I decided I'd try and get clean again, and this time I'd do it right.

Here I was, getting closer to forty, and still shooting up, even if it was only casually.

That's the first mistake, believing that heroin use can be casual. Maybe a very few can manage it, but not me. I'd learnt that the hard way. I don't believe I ever met anyone else who had managed it, either. Maybe the idea that it was possible was just an urban myth; something to use as an excuse for that extra shot.

PART ONE

GETTING IN 1983-1993

"Our national drug is alcohol. We tend to regard the use of any other drug with special horror."
~ William S. Burroughs

SO IT BEGINS

I began taking drugs when I was sixteen, and only got straight in my late thirties. I was one of the lucky ones. A lot of people I knew didn't make it through, lost in the hazy world of addiction and slow (or fast) death.

I started smoking dope before I finished high school, and progressed to amphetamines (speed or goey) fairly quickly. The majority of drug addicts are damaged goods, the ones who suffered abuse of some form and saw drugs as a way of coping with life or guilt.

I was one of the abused.

There was a teacher at primary school – I'll call him Mr Duffy – who took great pleasure in dishing out punishment to anyone who he saw as 'bad'. It didn't matter to him how small the infraction, he was ready to give them the strap: a wicked leather strip studded with metal. I always seemed to find myself in trouble, always seemed to be the one caught doing something wrong.

I found myself in the office at least three times a week, being punished for something.

I was about nine years old when it began.

At first, I thought he was just taking the punishment up a notch by strapping me on the bum instead of on the hand, but then he demanded I take my pants down.

One day I was caught fighting with another boy on the footy oval.

"Geoff, get into my office," Mr Duffy yelled.

I walked into his office. He followed me inside.

"Take down your pants and bend over the desk," he said. He took the strap out of his desk and moved over to close the curtains.

I did as he asked, shaking in terror.

Thwack. The first blow hurt more than it ever had before. I tried to push away from the desk, but he had one hand holding me by the neck as I struggled.

Thwack. It was harder this time. I screamed in pain.

"If you yell, I'll hurt you even more," he said.

I bit back my cries. I sobbed, gulping great lungfuls of air as I tried to get away from the pain.

I'm not sure what happened next, but I felt something soft and wet. "What are you doing?" I yelled, as I tried once more to turn around. He had hold of my jumper. His face was near my throbbing arse.

"Stop it," I yelled. He shook me.

"Shut up or I'll hurt you even worse, you little bastard."

I shut up, and he continued to lick the raised welts.

I felt his free hand move up my leg and between my thighs. He touched my penis, stroking it up and down.

I felt him stand up, and I heard him unbuckle his belt and drop his pants. He moved behind me and I felt something poking me as he took the hand away from my jumper and pushed me down flat onto the desk and raped me.

I'll never forget the pain and shame that I felt at that moment.

When he had finished, he told me to pull up my pants and get out.

'And don't ever think of telling anyone about this," he said. "No-one will ever believe you and you'll get into even more trouble than usual."

And so, for the next two years, I was raped at least once a week; sometimes more. He always seemed to be watching me, waiting for something he could punish me for.

I was quiet and withdrawn during these years. I was the odd one out, never really fitting in with the other kids. I was ashamed of what was happening to me, and the other kids somehow knew I had something to hide. Naturally, this singled me out for some 'special attention'.

Being bullied leaves scars; on the surface and deep

inside. I put up with it for a time before I finally cracked and fought back. I don't know why I left it for so long, but after I put up a fight, it stopped. The bullies looked elsewhere for easier targets. Eventually, even the other abuse stopped. I think Mr Duffy found another, younger, child to abuse. But the damage had been done. I wasn't the same person I had been before.

I had no brothers or sisters, having been adopted at six weeks by a couple who couldn't have their own children. I found out about the adoption at age sixteen, and have always wondered if perhaps this affected me subconsciously, due to the timing of my drug experimentation. I know I felt broken, empty, yet at the same time full of despair and pain at what had happened to me. I never found a way to talk about it, and even writing this brings back some of those same emotions, even though it's so far in the past and I'm a completely different person now than I was during the time I couldn't face up to the abuse and tried to find ways to mask it all.

I never lacked for material things. I had everything I could have wanted growing up. Everything except self-esteem and friends, that is.

I spent my youth in Sunshine, a working class suburb in the outer west of Melbourne filled with factories, working-class families, and take-away food outlets. There was nothing to do outside of school. Most days I ended up at home reading, or out with the few associates I did have, breaking into factories and smashing windows. If we weren't already in trouble, we were looking for ways to get into it.

The childhood abuse and bullying left me with a desire to learn how to fight, even though I felt too cowardly to do so most of the time, so I joined a local karate club. I studied there two nights a week for three years, then studied judo for two years after that, earning a bronze medal in the state championships while still a yellow belt. My final foray into martial arts was studying Wing Chun Gung Fu in a school in Melbourne's CBD, up to three classes a day with weights and wooden dummy practice in between. I vowed never to be a victim again. I didn't usually manage this, but there was always a line I never allowed people to cross. I just drew it too far back. I allowed myself to be the victim over and over again, even though I was more than capable of defending myself. For most of my life I thought it was fear that held me back, that I was a coward as well as a junkie and a useless piece of shit. Now, I realise I had been trained to be the victim during the abuse. I welcomed that feeling of being worthless, and I think I enjoyed being looked down at. I would sometimes run away from fights, and other times I'd let them hit me. If people thought I was gutless, that I had no heart, then maybe they'd just leave me alone. Stupid.

💉 💉 💉

I soon found some people to hang with, and after that I suffered less at the hands of the bullies that had made my life hell for so many years. In year ten of high school (1982), I became good friends with a girl in the new group named Carolyn – not the same one, but I seem to have a karmic attraction to the name. We used to go roller-skating together every week, and soon enough I became a fairly good skater.

Life became better, but still I was missing something; something felt wrong, absent from my life. I had a very low self-esteem, and had no luck with girls.

I felt I was in love with Carolyn, but I didn't have the nerve to act on it. I figured I was no good for anyone, and that no-one would ever want to be with me.

I spent all my spare time hanging around at her place, or going out with her. We did a lot of things a couple would do without ever actually being a couple.

This tore me apart inside, but I never let on how I felt. All I knew was that I wanted to spend as much time with her as possible. In the end, we were virtually inseparable. But I knew deep inside that girls wouldn't want me, so I never even tried.

Through Carolyn, who seemed to be attracted to the bad-boy type, I made a new group of friends and associates.

Above: Smoking a joint (stock image - not the author)

Below: Quality buds

SMOKIN' (1983)

Toward the end of high school, I was still best friends with Carolyn, still spending all my time with her. She had started dating guys, which was to be my downfall, both emotionally and physically. It really hurt to see her with someone else, holding hands or kissing in front of me. It was to lead me to something that would change my life forever.

My first experience with drugs was smoking marijuana at a party in 1983.

A guy Carolyn was seeing at the time, Steve, was the first to give me the opportunity to try marijuana. I was extremely jealous of him, and what he had with Carolyn, but he was a nice enough guy. Even though I hated the idea of him being with her, I found it hard to hate him as a person. We became friends.

Carolyn and Steve invited me over to the party one night. I spent the first hour or so moping around, trying to ignore those two holding hands, being boyfriend and girlfriend.

I'd had a couple of drinks by this stage, and when I walked into the kitchen, some guys were smoking dope at the table.

"Geoff... wanna cone?" Steve said.

"Um... I dunno."

"You've had dope before, haven't ya?" he asked.

"Uh... no," I said.

"D'ya wanna try it?"

To be honest, the idea scared the shit out of me, but at sixteen I needed to appear as a man, even though I didn't feel it. Even though I was a coward, or at least I thought I was, image in regard to fitting in was important to me.

Really, I was so damaged inside I couldn't see I was continually beating myself down. I thought that it was all I had.

I walked over and sat down, watching the guy sitting next to me smoke through a strange looking home-made thing, a combination of a fruit juice bottle and some plastic tubing.

Steve started to roll a joint. "If you've never tried it, it's easier on the lungs if you have a joint," he said.

Steve handed me the rollie. "This could be rough. Try not to cough."

I tried to light it with a match, but it just smouldered.

Steve laughed. "You have to suck on it to get it lit."

I lit another match, holding it to the tip of the joint as I sucked. It felt like knives tore at my throat and lungs, pain followed by a terrible taste.

I coughed so hard I thought one of my lungs had punctured as pain flared down my left side.

Finally, I got my breath back, and someone handed me back the joint, which I had accidentally dropped.

"Try and pull the smoke in your mouth, then breathe it back." I'm not sure who said this, my eyes still filled with tears. This time I managed to keep the smoke down, only coughing again once I'd breathed it out. It didn't hurt as much, but it didn't seem to be doing anything. I passed the joint to the next person and waited patiently for it to make its way around again.

We finished the joint but I didn't feel any different.

"Can I try a… a cone?" I asked.

Steve handed me the strange-looking thing. "It's called a 'bong'. Hold it like this," he said, "Then put your thumb over this hole while you suck in through the top and light the cone at the same time."

I tried to follow what he said, and managed to breathe in a lungful of smoke before I coughed down into the bong. Dirty water spurted out of the silver-foil cone where the dope burnt and everyone laughed at the mess.

"Not too bad for a first try," said Steve.

My head was spinning from the smoke, but after about five minutes this seemed to have more of an effect. I felt tired and dizzy, and just sat watching everyone around the table pulling cones, memorising the technique.

Eventually I found my way into a bedroom. I recall sitting on the bed for a second to gather my thoughts. After that, I remember very little else, just staring into nothing for what felt like a moment but in reality must have been hours. Carolyn came in and asked if I was okay. It seemed a silly question; I was fine – as fine as I could ever remember. At that moment, I realised how different I felt, how 'floaty' and happy and carefree.

This was good. For the first time in years, I felt sort of content. I felt *alive*.

I can't remember how I got home; I think maybe Carolyn's mum gave me a ride, or I may have walked. All I can remember is the next day thinking just how much I wanted to get high again.

Looking back, it still makes little sense to me. I can't be totally sure why I felt the need for drugs to make me happy. I've asked myself that question a million times. Maybe it was the sexual abuse and the need to suppress it. Maybe it was being adopted and never feeling close to my parents. I never came up with a definitive answer. I wish I knew then what I know now... maybe I could have told my parents what had been done to me, what was happening now, instead of hiding it from everyone. I could have begun to get some help rather than self-medicating.

Within weeks, I was smoking dope every weekend, and soon after that it became a daily occurrence. Dope was easy to get in Sunshine. During the eighties it wasn't policed as much as it is nowadays, if at all.

Around December of eighty-three I got to know a dealer in Wright Street who used to set up shop in his kitchen and serve customers out of the window that faced onto the driveway. People would line up, exchanging cash for foil-wrapped grams of dope, like a drive-thru window at McDonalds. Some nights, the line wound its way out his driveway and onto the footpath, spilling out into the real world, so to speak. Guys and girls stood around chatting and drinking while they waited to score. It was such a social event, and no-one bothered to try and be discreet.

In this day and age, no-one would dare be that blatant, but back then the cops either didn't know or didn't care. It was easier to obtain drugs than it was to get hold of alcohol. This suited my tastes perfectly. I didn't like drinking, so I smoked instead.

I smoked the Christmas of '83 away, and then I started on '84, my Year 12 at Sunshine High.

I had begun to withdraw from my family after primary school, spending more and more time alone in my bedroom. I had a television, a good stereo and a video-recorder, so I didn't have to socialise. I don't know why my parents didn't push me to be more social and to sit in the lounge-room with them. I think that being adopted, we had all failed to bond fully, the way a normal family does from birth, although I never had any doubts they loved me, and I loved them, too. I know I felt worse being alone all the time, but I was scared to try and do things and find nothing but rejection. I could get lost in my books, music and TV shows, they never hurt me or made me feel less than everyone else. I would read about kids who succeeded, who had true friends, and didn't fail at having another human being love them for who they were, like I did. It gave me an escape and it gave me the opportunity to get stoned all the time without them noticing.

I used to roll joints and go out to the street to smoke. I made sure the neighbours didn't see, and I made sure I used cologne to mask the smell.

My parents used to go away on weekends to markets and run a stall selling vintage jewellery and linen and assorted collectibles. Once I was old enough to look after myself, they'd leave me home alone. This coincided perfectly with the beginning of my descent into drugs. It gave me the freedom to indulge myself every weekend. I had a chip on my shoulder and a terrible case of nearly no self-esteem, and without knowing it, a deep-seated anger and resentment over the abuse I'd suffered when I was younger. The marijuana gave me a break from those unwanted feelings.

It was around this time I began studying judo in St Albans to learn different fighting skills, which is where I met Chris A.

Chris became a good friend. His older brother, Marek, was the dojo instructor. It didn't take long before Chris and I hung together most weekends and smoked dope. He was a nice guy with a heart of gold, a shitload of loyalty and a great sense of fun.

We'd scored some Lebanese Gold hashish, a stronger version of marijuana made from the oils of the plant. We mulled it up (a strange mix of heating and rubbing into tobacco) and had some bongs. Chris ran outside to the laundry to throw up, not used to the strength of the drug.

I was sitting in the lounge, listening to Pink Floyd at full volume. The album intro was playing, a loud and realistic heartbeat, when suddenly the back door slammed open.

"*Fuck*! I'm dying. My heart's gonna explode!" Chris staggered into the lounge room, a stricken look on his pale face. Eyes wide and scared as hell, he lurched over to lean against the mantelpiece.

"What the fuck you talkin' about?" I asked, laughing.

"I... I can hear my heart, it's about to explode," he stammered.

"Dude, that's on the stereo," I said, a grin on my face.

"Wha...?" he asked.

"It's Pink Floyd, man. *Dark Side of the Moon*. You know, the part with the heartbeat," I said.

"Oh... yeah... I knew that," he replied, a relieved look on his face.

We had another pipe each and settled into listening to the album as loud as my stereo could play it.

Stoned again.

Apart from school, it soon became my main mission in life to get off my face as often as possible. Then I began to crave the pipe when I was at school. Dope became my life-support. I definitely preferred dope to drinking. Drinkers can be loud, obnoxious and brutal, or morose, passive-aggressive and violent. I had my joints, and on the weekend I could smoke a bong, so I was happy.

CARSICK (1984)

After I discovered dope, I participated less at home and at school, although my grades rarely suffered. I had no trouble with the work side of school, but behaviour and engagement certainly dropped. I tried and tried to feel like I fitted in, but I just couldn't get past my constant fear. I studied to be a fighter, yet was too scared to fight. I think the anxiety that came on through confrontation reminded me too much of my victimisation at the hands of the teacher.

I partied every weekend, and spent way too much on dope. My parents seemed content to let me sit in my room and read, but maybe they just felt unsure of what to say or do to bring me out of my funk. All I know is that Dad worked long hours as a fitter and turner, Mum looked after the house, and they both left me alone as much as I wanted but more than I needed. I tried to smother my feelings under a cloud of smoke. It was getting expensive, especially for a student. Dad would slip me spending money from the markets, but I needed to either cut down smoking or find another way to get stoned.

Looking around for a cheaper high, I soon discovered that one brand of motion sickness tablets brought on major hallucinations when taken in much larger doses than recommended. They weren't that expensive and I could get them over-the-counter without any awkward questions.

The standard dose for motion sickness was one tablet, but people knew that if you took all ten in the pack you would start to hallucinate quite severely. Taken with a couple of bourbons or a joint, they'd last about twelve hours.

I was walking home from a mate's place after a party, off my face on these tabs, and I encountered an old guy, a bum, lying asleep across the footpath. He appeared transparent, outlined in fluorescent colours. I stepped over him and he disappeared.

Another time, walking home from West Sunshine across Kororoit Creek, I had to jump over a garden fence to avoid fifty-foot spiders. I rolled over to find that the spiders weren't there, and neither was the fence. The tablets were working well.

They made you feel like shit the next day, like being poisoned, but the twelve-hour trip seemed worth it. On the days I was straight, I kept reliving the abuse. I couldn't move on. All I could do was take drugs to try and block out the memories. It worked, because after a few years, I no longer thought about it, or even remembered until I got off all the stuff a long time later.

I didn't even begin to consider the social, physical and mental damage that could occur as a result of taking all these different drugs, and at seventeen, I don't think I would have cared. Aren't we all bulletproof when we're young and dumb?

Charmed life, ten feet tall, nothing can happen to me.

At the same time, I believe I was giving myself what I thought I deserved.

*   *   *

The south side of Sunshine, over the train line and overpass that separated the suburb, housed the police station and the main hang-outs for teenagers in the 80s. The coolest places had pool tables and noisy slot machines; old men sitting and drinking Turkish coffee in the back room while noisy teenagers strutted in the front amidst the lights and the noise.

The smaller upstairs arcade just past Tony's Pizza Parlour was the home of the younger criminal set around Sunshine.

Drugs were sold there, robberies and acts of violence were plotted and all sorts of rorts were either planned or recruited for, out of sight of the cops.

Tony's was also a favourite hangout, but much more relaxed than the game arcade upstairs. Old Tony ran the pizza parlour, while his son, Tony Jnr, ran the counter and cooked. Tony's was also a favourite of the suburban godfathers who played out Al Pacino day and night. Endless pizzas delivered to tables up the back, cappuccino after cappuccino consumed in dark and smoky corners. It was like a low budget Tarantino movie.

Throughout '83, I hung mostly at Tony's, and became great friends with Tony Jnr, who was always sending our table a free pizza loaded with extra cheese. It was a great time.

We had a particularly unusual associate who used to always raise our spirits during that time. Every day, Maurice would come in from Maidstone on the public transport system, always in a costume even though he must have been in his twenties, and just hang around in the pinball arcade or the pizza joint. He was very simple, but a nice guy and always happy. If you did manage to get on the wrong side of him, though, watch out.

One fine Friday afternoon, Maurice stepped down from the Met bus, cowboy hat and western shirt and boots, wearing spurs and chaps, with two plastic cap guns on a dress-up gunbelt. He hitched up his pants and stepped off the curb to cross over City Place towards Tony's. A car engine gunned and tyres screamed as a small hatchback swerved towards him, guys hanging out front and back windows on the passenger side.

"Move it, you fucking freak. What's wrong with you?" one screamed. "Playing dress-up or are you just fucked in the head?"

Laughing, the driver screeched to a stop only inches from Maurice's legs.

Now, Maurice was a big, muscly guy, even though his brain wasn't fully developed, and as he stepped around towards the driver, the laughter slowed, then stopped. Up close, he must have looked a lot more intimidating than they first thought. He swept off his cowboy hat, his shiny, shaven head glistening with sweat in the sun.

"Why you tease me?" Maurice said. "Why you *mean* to me?"

He reached through the open drivers' window, grabbed the guy by the shirt, and dragged him half out of his window.

"Why you mean to me?" he screamed as he slapped the driver over and over. The other two guys spilled out of the car, moving towards Maurice. By this time, a few people had run from the pinball arcade and grabbed Maurice, pulling him away. The three from the car jumped back inside and took off, tires screaming and abuse flying from open windows.

Another day in Sunshine.

SHOOTING GALLERY (1984)

I began my hard-drug abuse with methamphetamine, sometimes called speed or goey, and more recently found in much higher purity and called ice. Unlike most users, I didn't bother ever snorting or drinking it. The first time I ever tried speed I went for the fastest and most efficient way of using and injected it, aka shot it up. Well, someone else shot me up. I had no idea how it was going to feel.

Luke was a part-time friend from primary school.

We'd been good friends when he was the new kid arriving in grade two. I was the first friend he had there. We were pretty inseparable, but a few years later, things changed.

He started to hang with the bullies; started making weaker kids' lives hell. This went on through the first four years of high school as well, but in the last two years, he finally grew up. I was smoking dope at this point, and so was he, so we tended to turn up to the same druggie parties.

Soon enough, I started to hang around with him and his mates at the local squash court. He worked there part-time.

We had some wild times, and a lot of drugs were taken.

Through Luke I met Darren, his dope dealer. Short and stocky, he had long dark hair and a fuzzy growth on his upper lip and chin.

Darren's nickname was Oz. He was a part-time smoker and speed user. He made a decent living by selling much more of both than he ever used himself. He always had a sleepy look to him, as though he had just woken up.

My first ever taste of speed was with Oz, who lived in a small bungalow at the back of a house about three blocks from my place in Perth Avenue. I bought bud from Darren, but one night he offered me something different.

"Hey," said Darren. "I just got a quarter ounce of speed. Wanna try it?"

"Sure," I said. "What's it do?"

"It makes you feel alive, and everything is more fun."

He moved off into one of the two bedrooms. About a minute later he returned with a small piece of folded silver foil.

"It's fifty bucks for a gram, or twenty-five for a half gram," he said.

"Gimme a gram of it," I said, pulling a fifty out of my wallet and passing it over. "How do I take it? Do I sniff it up?"

"Well, you can, but it's better if you inject it."

I stopped cold.

"Inject?" I said. "I've never done that before. Wouldn't know how to."

"That's fine," Darren said. "I can do it for you."

He went over to the bench that separated the lounge area from the tiny kitchen, and pulled a spoon from a drawer. Ran a tap to fill a glass with cold water, and pulled a sealed one-use syringe out of another drawer.

I watched in silence as he opened up the foil package and gently tapped out about half of the white powder into the spoon. He opened the package the syringe was in and removed the orange cap that covered the needle. I watched closely as, dipping it into the glass of water he pulled the plunger back and drew some into the chamber, then held up the syringe to check how much was in there. He flicked the syringe with a finger, getting an air bubble up to the top, and then carefully pushed the plunger so water streamed out the tip of the needle and the amount in the chamber showed as 50, roughly half of the syringe.

Darren squirted the water into the spoon, and we both watched as the speed dissolved into nothing, leaving behind a tiny residue on the bottom of the dessert spoon. Darren grabbed a cigarette lighter and heated the bottom of the spoon for a few seconds, swirling carefully so no liquid spilled, then grabbed a cigarette. He tore a small piece of filter away, dropped it into the spoon, then used the syringe to suck up all the liquid through the filter.

He turned to me. "Right, get up your sleeve on the right arm," he said.

I did, and laid my arm on the bench. He proceeded to tap the inside crook of my elbow, then slid the needle into the visible vein. It stung for a second, then he drew back on the plunger and I marvelled at the burst or bright red blood that appeared inside the chamber. He pressed down, pushing the speed into my bloodstream, then pulled out the needle. Blood oozed, so I wiped it away from the hole in my arm.

Suddenly my head exploded, or felt like it, anyway.

It felt like lightning had struck my chest, a jolt of electricity travelling from the top of my head to the soles of my feet. Sweat broke out all over me, and my eyes nearly popped out.

This was *fantastic!*

Everything was clear, a complete, total and perfect clarity of vision and thought. I felt great. I felt good about myself for the first time. This sure felt like a great thing.

I still stuck with smoking, as the speed was an expensive alternative, but man, did I like the feeling it gave me. I soon enough learnt where to buy syringes, and how to shoot myself up. It was a messy training period, but I soon got very good at it.

My life was about to change for the worse, and I have Oz and a guy I hadn't yet met to thank for giving me the opportunity to become less than I was meant to be.

I first met Gary at Tony's Pizza around August of '84. He was older than the crowd in the front section. This gave him an allure, especially since he was a known drug user and a bit of a local standover man.

He drove a truck for a Sunshine towing firm, back in the days before the towing allocation system. Back then, it was the first truck to the scene of the accident that got the job, and those guys could drive. Once a few trucks arrived, there were plenty of fights between drivers to decide who was getting the job. All in all it was a rough business to be in.

Gary seemed a decent enough guy. We got along well, so he invited me over to his place, a caravan in Tottenham Gates Caravan Park.

I'd go over most days and hang around with him and his wife. We'd sit and listen to the cop channels on a police radio scanner, trying to get a heads-up on any local crashes.

It was September 1984, and I was seventeen. I remember being at a house in Braybrook, a western suburbs Housing Commission area.

Gary was the common denominator between me, the guy whose house it was (Sam) and a lot more of the speed I'd come to enjoy. Gary knew the guy who sold bulk, I didn't. Gary had arranged to buy an ounce for Sam, and he'd been given some of the gear for arranging the buy.

I was in his bathroom, leaning against the wall with my right arm held out, tied off with a skipping rope. My sleeve was rolled up so that he could get the tip of the syringe into the vein. It slid under the skin, less painfully than some of my own attempts, but it missed the first time, and the second as well. The third try he managed to strike a vein.

As he pulled gently on the plunger, I saw the red blood balloon into the chamber, reminding me of a lava lamp the way it bloated and grew. I felt dizzy. My knees went a little weak. He motioned for me to remove the rope and then pressed down on the plunger, the burgeoning blossom of blood disappearing like an explosion shown in reverse, injecting the high-quality speed straight into my bloodstream.

I don't remember much from the rest of that night, it was all a blur of conversation.

At some point, we went for a drive in the tow-truck. My head was full of pins and needles, and I hung it out the window to feel the wind on my scalp. It was the first time I could remember being totally carefree and maybe even happy. This stuff was heaven.

I'd been hooked straight away. I wanted – needed – to hold onto this feeling. I felt like it fixed every problem I'd had. It even gave me a few hours where I didn't think about Mr Duffy.

Like any drug-fueled suburb, Richmond's alleys are littered with decay and syringes

GARY (1984-85)

I was shooting up speed more and more. Sometimes with Darren, and sometimes with Gary. I think my parents may have suspected something was up, but I kept to myself more and more, staying holed up in my room when I was home, which was becoming rarer and rarer. My mum accused me of using the place as a motel, coming home every second or third night for a shower and to sleep. I didn't care. My folks chose to just let me be, maybe hoping I'd sort out whatever problems I had by myself. It was almost as if they didn't care (although I now know they did) and that was fine by me. It gave me the freedom I needed to spend more and more time at Gary's place, doing drugs.

We smoked dope through a massive Galliano bottle that had been converted into a bong. It was smooth, and when you sat down you had to stand it on the floor between your feet to use it.

There was always hash around in those days, especially around the end of the year. Good Lebanese Gold or red cellophane gear from the Middle East. We'd get so smashed we couldn't even walk, and then we'd have a whack of speed to straighten up for a ride in the tow-truck when there was news of a crash on the scanner.

Gradually, Gary introduced me to using on a daily basis. I'd have a whack in the caravan, enjoy the speed rush while it lasted and then go to the toilet block and have a crap, which would bring on another rush of sensation, nearly as good as when you first had the gear.

I was still finishing high school, always speeding or stoned on hash or both.

I wasn't eating or sleeping properly. I'd always been bulky, but now I was shedding weight like I was sick.

We'd go out in the tow-truck to any nearby accidents, racing along the streets well over the speed limit.

I remember speeding along Sunshine Road, siren screaming and lights flashing into the night. It was raining. The water on the road reflected the colours a million times over as we roared along at a hundred kilometres an hour. As we approached West Footscray, we saw more flashing lights: blue, red and orange. The cops were already there, and so was another tow-truck. One of the Footscray drivers had beaten us to the wreck.

It was a nasty smash. A Ford Falcon had skidded in the wet and driven straight through the front of a shop. The car's roof – and the driver's head – had been torn off by a road-sign he'd collected on the way.

The car was stuck nose first in the shop; broken glass and rubble littered all around. The torn roof lay scattered over the road and the driver's severed head sat in the middle of the intersection.

As we pulled up, one of the cops pulled a white cloth out of the boot of his car and covered the head.

We stood around for twenty minutes doing nothing, and eventually went back to Gary's caravan and had some more cones.

💉 💉 💉

It was getting closer to Christmas of '84, and I'd nearly finished year twelve. Gary had been financing a lot of the drug use so far, but now that I was using every day he pointed out that I had to start putting in more often than I could afford to right then. Don't get me wrong, I was spending every cent I could get on drugs, but I only had a part-time job at Wendy's Burgers, so it wasn't enough to finance a full-time habit. It wasn't fair on him or Julie, he told me.

It was also around this time that Gary said we needed to go for a drive up to Shepparton to pick up a friend's kid, a seventeen year old named Kevin. He'd gotten mixed up with the wrong crowd, taking drugs and doing burglaries. His father decided to straighten him out by sending him down to Melbourne and into the hands of Gary. Not a great decision at all, as it was only going to get worse.

Within a day, we were all shooting up together and trying to work out how to raise some more cash.

Business, residential, and drug-based lifestyles all mix in Richmond's side streets. Each set of circumstances brings its own flavour to the suburb's thoroughfares.

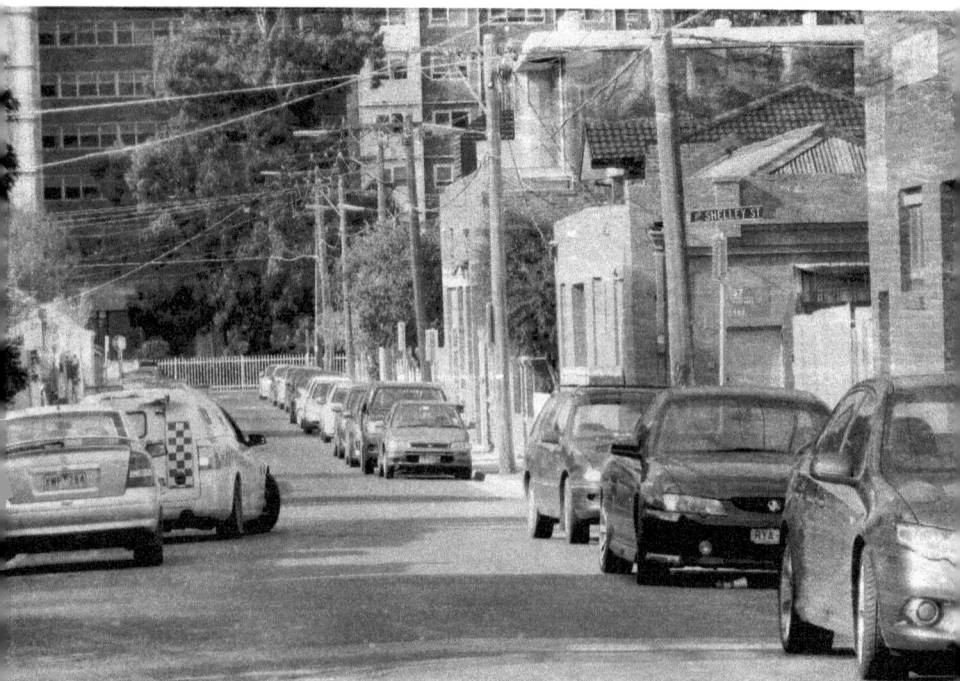

THIEF (END OF 1985)

Early in November, Gary made a mix with some nice hash and shouted us a blast of speed. As usual, it was high-quality. The headrush hit me while I was still pushing down on the plunger: I suddenly felt warm, and had tingles all over.

We waited for the rush to die down and started smoking hash.

"How do you guys plan on covering your share of the drug bill?" Gary asked.

I looked at Kevin and then back to Gary, unsure of how to answer. "I... I could get another job, I guess?"

"It'd have to be a fuckin' good job," Gary said. "We're using a couple of hundred bucks worth of gear a week between us. Add the smoko and it's close to five hundred you two owe me for the last coupl'a weeks. An' that ain't includin' before then, either."

"What the fuck can I do?" I asked.

"We can do a few jobs to raise some cash," Gary said.

"What d'ya mean?" Kevin asked.

"We can do a few burgs, seein' as it's so close to Chrissy," Gary answered. "There'll be new shit laying around in houses everywhere, ready for pressies. Just waiting to be taken."

"I'll be in that," Kevin said.

"I dunno, mate," I said. "Seems pretty shitty stealing presents."

"It's that or you can fuck off and buy your own gear," Gary said.

"Yeah... fine... I guess so,' I said. I felt like shit even saying it.

I'd never done anything like that before, and I didn't really like the idea. I sure as hell didn't want to stop shooting up, though. I didn't think I really had a choice, so I went along with it.

💉 💉 💉

Nicely-kept and tidy, the darkened house looked like it belonged to some affluent yuppies. We hoped there'd be a load of cash there too.

Kevin moved to the front door and tried the handle while I checked out the windows to see if any were left open. No such luck.

The place looked good. Some immigrants, especially out in the western suburbs, didn't trust banks. They kept all their money at home. With some luck, we'd find a wad of cash and not have to lug heavy electronics out to the car.

I walked over to the front door, keeping to the shadows. I pulled a screwdriver from my back pocket and moved Kevin out of the way. I jammed the blade in as close to the lock as I could. I wiggled it a bit, and then applied some leverage. It gave pretty easily.

I went straight to the back door and unlocked it just in case we needed an escape route. Then, carefully listening for noises, I moved down the hallway to the bedrooms while Kevin scoped the lounge. Deep down I knew this was wrong – more wrong than my usual shit.

I started looking in the main bedroom. My pulse was racing and I was sweating. I rifled through the drawers, hoping for a stash of cash. I found an old gold watch with a broken band but no sign of any money.

I left the room after jamming the watch into my pocket and made my way back to the lounge. I could make out the darker shape of Kevin on his hands and knees, checking out the contents of a sideboard.

"Dude," I whispered. "I got a watch but no cash. Any luck?"

"Nothing. I've unplugged the tellie and the video. Did you find anything else?" he asked.

"Nah," I said. "Let's just get the fuck out of here."

I left Kevin there while I slipped carefully out the front and down the street to where Gary had parked the car. It was a station wagon, with plenty of room in the back. I tried to stay out of the streetlights as I went.

I reached the car, but there was no sign of Gary. I jumped a mile when he appeared out of the bushes nearby.

"What's the go, Geoff?" he asked.

"We got a tellie and video player, but there's fuck-all else. I grabbed a gold watch as well," I replied.

"Is that it?" he said.

"Yep. Let's go... Kev'll have the shit ready by now." I hopped into the passenger side while Gary jumped behind the wheel. He started the car, fumbling with the keys

The car started with a rattle, and we pulled out into the street, lights off. We cruised quietly to the driveway and reversed in.

"I'll keep watch, you guys get the stuff," Gary said.

"No worries," I replied. I moved to the front door as Kevin opened it, video player in his arms.

I moved past him and waited for him to run back so we could lift the TV between us. It was a big one, and heavy as fuck.

After we loaded it, I jumped in the front seat as Kevin threw himself into the back.

It was only once we got a couple of blocks away with no sign of pursuit that Gary switched the headlights on and we all breathed a little easier. We'd be in Footscray in twenty minutes. We knew a guy who bought stolen goods anytime of the day or night. He'd ran a profitable business for years out of his flat above a shop in the east end of the shopping strip.

Soon enough, we had nearly two hundred bucks in cash for the video and TV. I didn't like doing the burglary, but I sure liked the drugs we bought with the proceeds.

The thing was, I couldn't get past the nagging doubts I had about how wrong it was to do shit like that. I started to drift away from Gary and Kevin, and, around the same time, I went back to another source of speed that let me cut those two out of my life completely.

OZ (1986)

'd finished school, and at this point I was hanging with Oz more and more and Gary less and less. Oz lived with his girlfriend, Belinda, and two Rottweilers who had the run of the yard. He had to install an intercom system on the front gate so that he could go out and bring people inside. Belinda's brother Joe and I were the only two people the dogs would let jump the fence and knock on the door.

Joe was a nice guy but a hopeless speed addict who loved two things: amphetamines and motorcycles.

I'd moved out of home for a short while by this time, living with Julie and Pommy, two friends. I hung with Oz, shooting up every day and working like a demon at any job I could find. At one stage I worked two different jobs, one nine-till-five at a locksmith doing master-keying systems, the other at the Footscray wholesale fruit and vegie markets with Pommy, looking for cash-in-hand work unloading trucks and semis. The smaller fruit and veg would be pre-loaded and shipped in pallet containers, but the larger stuff, like pumpkins and watermelons, would be loose within the fenced cargo trailer of a semi. We'd climb up into the bed, standing on top of the produce, and the forklift would raise two pallets to the top of the load and we'd start filling them. It usually took the two of us about two hours to empty one trailer (I think they carried about 35 tonnes of fruit or veg) and we'd get paid $250 cash for the job. At $125 each for two hours' work, and us working about eight hours a night, we'd average about $500 each every night, pretty good money for the mid-1980s.

That work would last through until around six, then we'd go and have a massive breakfast at the nearby truck-stop. After eating, I'd race to score some more speed and start the whole cycle over. It was tough.

I think I managed this for about three months before I just couldn't do it any more, even with the aid of the speed. I knew things had to change, but I didn't know how.

I quit unloading trucks, moved back home with the folks, spent more time with Oz, sometimes testing his speed when he got a new batch. You never knew what each delivery would be like. Drug-fucked bikies and career criminals aren't the most trustworthy chemists, after all.

The labs I'd seen weren't exactly run to any health standards. Speed was and always will be a gutter drug.

TRIPPIN'

Speed and dope weren't the only drugs I used. I was willing to try anything, the cheaper the better. It was about four in the morning. I was on a road-trip to Castle Falls with Joe and Oz to collect a load of magic mushrooms. Goldtops grew there in great numbers. The trick was to wait for a forecast of sunny weather in the middle of a particularly cold snap. Frost overnight combined with a nice sunny day were the perfect conditions for goldtops to grow.

We arrived just before dawn, which left us just enough time to have a couple of bongs first.

I looked around the car at the other two. "This is gonna be awesome. It's fucking cold, though."

Oz finished making the mix and grabbed the bong out. All I could see through the condensation and steam covering the windows were the vague shadows of trees surrounding the car-park.

Oz had a bong and passed me the next one. I lit up, breathing in the harsh smoke. I held it in for a few seconds and breathed out slowly. It hurt a little – it was the first pipe of the day – but I managed not to cough.

Joe opened his door and got out to stretch his legs. "C'mon, guys. Let's get going. I want some fuckin' mushies."

"Hold up, Joe. Let's have another cone before we go," Oz said. We smoked another round and then got out. It was freezing. Our breath steamed in front of us as we walked over to the edge of the car park. There was a low fence with some small gumtrees just past it, and then the roar of the water from the falls. We moved to the edge of the river.

Careful not to slip or lose our balance, we crossed over the shallows, using rocks that poked above the swirling water

We made it to the other side without a slip, and made our way up the hill. The sky was just starting to lighten as the sun rose in the east. I lit a cigarette and we waited at the top for enough light to see the ground. It was fucking freezing, but it'd be worth it to get off our faces on mushies.

We spent the next two hours filling shopping bags with mushrooms, collecting about three hundred and fifty goldtops. The fresh young buttontops were the best, so we threw out the big ones that were a couple of days old and ended up with about two hundred and fifty buttons.

Before we left to go home, we had another mix in the car. Joe and I had a few mushies straight out of the bag at the same time. They tasted how you'd expect; like chewing on a lump of mould. The hardest thing was keeping them down.

Just as we got through the nearest town, the mushies started to work.

At first, I felt like my head had been stuffed with cotton wool. I felt nauseous and my stomach felt bloated. Soon, the cotton-head feeling went away, and I felt electrified. My senses seemed overpowered. Things were louder and brighter than normal, and the sunlight made my eyes weep. I had no sunglasses with me; a bad mistake.

"Fuck, guys... I'm trippin' here," I said.

The mushies made me feel all hazy and a bit nauseous. For the rest of the drive, everything took on a new look. It seemed like something out of a Dr Seuss book: high piles of rocks and trees that drooped too much to be normal.

Once we arrived back at Oz's place, we boiled up the remaining mushies and made cups of Milo with the disgusting brew. All up, I probably had close to a hundred mushrooms that day, at least eight or nine times the amount needed to get off. I remember very little of the next two days, except for sitting on the floor, limp and tripping, watching the colours on the walls move into strange and wonderful patterns. Oz later told me that I pissed myself –

not realising I needed to go to the toilet – and that Jerry had run around screaming for hours that the couch had grown arms and was trying to kill him. After that, I pretty much lost interest in mushies.

✒ ✒ ✒

Oz rang me up one day and asked if I wanted to go out shooting with him and a guy named Phil we knew from Sunshine. I assumed he meant rifles or shotties, but when I arrived at his place there were three handguns sitting on the table. I was excited, never having shot a pistol before.

There was a .38 revolver, a .44 magnum revolver, and a 9mm semi-automatic. We drove past the outskirts of Melbourne, up towards Ballarat, until we found a road that led deep into the bush. We parked about three kilometres from the highway, and went for a walk into the forest.

Except for the .44, the pistols weren't as loud as I'd expected.

We picked up every casing – we didn't want to risk leaving any behind with our prints all over them.

We shot trees and cans and bottles for the rest of the day and went home once it got dark. It was a hell of a day, which I'll always remember, and we used a hell of a lot of ammo.

SPEED FREAK (1986-87)

Soon enough, I was back to using heaps of speed, about a quarter ounce each week. By this stage, I was run down. I wasn't sleeping much and, when I did, I just woke up craving more speed. I was hungry all the time, but I couldn't eat anything without throwing it back up again. I had to do something before I became as starved and as strung out as Joe. Around this time I met another of Oz's friends, a short, skinny guy named Sean. He smoked dope and shot-up speed as much as I did. Soon enough, we became friends.

I was still living with my folks again at this point. When I used at home, I stashed my syringes behind my desk. I think the folks must have suspected I was on drugs, but I didn't know for sure until I got home from Oz's one day.

I walked into the house to find Mum and Dad sitting at the kitchen table. Mum was crying.

"What's wrong?" I asked.

"Follow me," Dad said, getting up from the table and walking down the hall toward my room.

Oh shit.

The desk had been pulled away from the wall and dozens of syringes were piled up on the floor behind it.

"What are they?" he asked.

I didn't know what to say.

"What have you been doing?" Dad looked shrunken with sorrow.

"I have a friend who's diabetic," I said. I knew it sounded stupid, but I didn't know what else to say.

"Don't lie to me," he said.

I was speeding, so I thought I'd be able to talk my way out of this one.

"It's Luke. He's had diabetes for over a year." I knew it sounded like a lie, but I couldn't think of anything else. There was no way I'd admit to being a druggie.

Mum came down to the room, still crying. I couldn't face them anymore. I walked out and started looking for a place to stay. They didn't say a word when I left, so I figured they didn't really care.

I ended up at Sean's.

He was living in a ramshackle bungalow out the back of a house occupied by two alcoholics in North Sunshine.

Four two-roomed bungalows were crowded together in a run-down back yard. They all shared the same shower and toilet and a sheltered area with three torn-up armchairs and a pool table. The rooms were shabby and sparse, full of dangerous power-points and scuffed plasterboard. Someone had thrown them together just to make a few bucks from illegal tenants.

A week later, I moved into one of the other bungalows when the occupant died.

The people who lived there were pretty fucked-up. Rachel and Barry, a junkie couple, lived in the front right-hand bungalow. He was always stealing shit to buy speed, and he beat the crap out of her regularly.

I was in the front left-hand side, and an old alcoholic named Chris lived in the place behind mine. I think he used to fuck the Labrador he kept as a pet. The noises I heard suggested more than a normal relationship. The only person I really mixed with was Sean, behind Barry and Rachel's place. He worked at a tow-truck company in Deer Park, but quit about a week after I moved in. I ended up getting his job there.

I was in charge of the two-way radio used to communicate with the tow-truck drivers, and responsible for taking allocation calls from the Road Traffic Authority. I worked there for about four months until I was caught stealing. The owner, John, ran a cash-only register in the section where my desk was. The register was an old one, and there was never a roll of paper in there to record transactions. A load of the cash was never declared: John would just come in at the end of the day and take at least half out and stuff it in his shirt pocket. At the time, I was using as much speed as I could afford, although it was never enough. I had a heated internal debate for all of thirty seconds.

I waited until everyone was on lunch and opened the till. There was at least a grand there, mostly in fifties. I grabbed three of them and quietly shut the till. I turned around to find Jack, the second in charge, staring at me from outside the door. He turned away and I stuffed the money down my balls and went back to lunch. The schnitzel I was eating suddenly didn't taste so good, but all I could think of was scoring as soon as I finished work. Later that day, John came in to talk to me.

"Get the fuck out of here," he said. "You're fired." I left without a backward glance – straight to Oz's place. I never told anyone what had happened. I was too ashamed. Like always, even when I was a little kid in the lolly shop, I knew stealing was wrong.

At this point I was worthless, and life was worthless. I lost all will to live, and one day I decided to end it. Just end it and give up. Finish what my choices up until now had started.

I stuffed rags under all the doors and in the gaps in the windows, and turned the gas stove on, along with all the burners. I didn't light them, figuring going to sleep and being gassed would be fairly painless.

I sat down on the bed, then leant back onto the pillows and closed my eyes, scared to die but even more scared to live. I kept having flashbacks to the abuse I'd suffered when I was a kid. I relived everything. I went through all the old pain, the humiliation, how I truly believed it was my fault, not his. I'd done something to ask for it. I'd led him on. I'd done something bad that no-one else had done, and that was why he'd done it. I was a failure. I had nothing to offer anyone, least of all myself. I'd never had a real relationship, and to be honest, I felt unworthy of ever being loved. How could anyone love someone like me? I was damaged goods, and I would never be whole again.

Three hours later I woke up, still alive even with gas all through the unit, but obviously not enough to kill me. I couldn't even do that right.

I grabbed a syringe, filled it with air, and injected it. This would have to kill me, wouldn't it? Everyone knew air bubbles caused brain damage and people died from it.

Nope. That failed too.

There wasn't anything I could do right, so I even gave up on ending it all. I may as well just enjoy the drugs while I could, and not care about anything.

Sean moved out to a rented house in West Footscray to grow marijuana with Oz. I stayed in the bungalow for another three months until they finished a crop, then I moved in with Sean. It was around this time that I bought a cheap electric guitar and started to learn how to play.

The place was a semi-detached on Geelong Road. The two bedrooms both had badly stained carpets, soiled in rings where the pot plants had stood. There was a musty, mouldy smell all the time, especially in the wet months. I don't think Darren or Sean took very good care of the place when they were growing dope there.

I settled into a routine of smoking every day and using speed as often as I could. This went on for at least a year. I knew I should stop using, but I didn't know how. When I tried to go without for a few days, the memories of abuse kept coming back, mostly in dreams. I was a wreck, on speed, but I just didn't know how to cope without it. At that point, I gave up thinking about getting straight and kept on using as much as I could.

Every day it was the same thing.

"Hey man, wanna score?" Sean was cooking toast. We had nothing to put on it, so it was always dry toast.

"Sure do," I replied. Just the thought of having a whack of speed made my gut tighten in anticipation. "Oz won't be up yet, but he should be by the time we drive there. I'll jump in the shower and we can head off, if you want?"

"No worries, man. I'll make a mix. There'll be a cone waiting by the time you finish," Sean said with a grin as he pulled the bowl from under the couch.

Soon enough we were stoned and driving, Pink Floyd on the tape deck and windows down. We made it to Oz's around eleven, and pulled up outside.

I jumped the fence while Sean waited out the front. Oz's two Rottweilers would have eaten him if he'd tried going over the fence with me. As I got to the front door, it opened. Belinda stood there, coffee in hand.

'Hey Geoff. Wassup?' She moved aside and opened the door all the way.

"Sean's at the gate."

Belinda put the dogs inside, then turned and pressed a button underneath the intercom, which opened the gate. Sean walked down the drive.

I followed her inside, telling Sean to shut the door behind him. Oz was just up, in his undies and a grungy t-shirt on the sofa with a coffee in front of him. He was barely awake. He reminded me of the sheep-dog in the Warner Brothers cartoons – hair over his eyes and half-asleep.

"G'day, boys," he said with his usual half-smirk. Sean sat down next to him on the sofa, while I sat on the armchair. Belinda went out to the kitchen to watch tellie while we did our drug shit. I always got the feeling she was never happy about the whole thing. She didn't use drugs herself, and didn't like Oz using them either, unless it was just a bong or two.

"Can I grab a bit of goey, mate?" Sean asked.

"Me too," I added quickly.

Oz smirked even more and just looked at us, waiting for us to ask again. He loved playing God with the people who wanted to buy gear. Because he only used occasionally, he thought himself better than the ones he saw as hopeless junkies. In retrospect, I think he was so much worse.

I sighed, eager to get this part of the game over and done with. "So can we get some or not?" I asked.

Oz grinned at me, and then grumbled something under his breath. But he did get up and start moving. He disappeared into the bedroom for a few minutes before he returned with two foil wraps, a gram of gear for each of us. "On the bill, guys?"

"Yep," we both said.

"It's getting up a bit now, for both of ya." Oz liked to bring up details like this in public. I think it made him feel better to make us look – and feel – worse.

We went into the bathroom to mull up the gear, grabbing a spoon each on the way. Soon enough, we were rushing off our heads, sitting around with Oz, watching him play guitar and smoking more dope. Another day in 'paradise'.

I spent the next year bumming around, not really working. I used a shit-load of drugs, though. I knew in the back of my mind that it couldn't go on, yet there seemed to be no way out. I needed to be speeding or stoned to keep the memories from driving me insane. It ate away at me when I was straight. So did the fact that I was using so many drugs.

I guess I knew deep down that I just couldn't go on, but if I refused to face it – if I kept on using as many drugs as I could afford – then I could be stoned enough to ignore it.

Not an easy year for me, although I did get a very cool birthday present from the parents. An electric guitar and amplifier, along with a couple of effects pedals I picked out. Now I could do something with my time spent speeding. Play guitar all night.

It was early '87 when the folks decided to move to the country. I thought that it'd be a lot quieter drug-wise in rural Victoria. Maybe I needed to get away from it all, get away from the speed and get away from the friends I hung with.

I'd been seeing Mum and Dad off-and-on since I left home. They knew I was fucked up, but I don't think they could bring themselves to abandon me. About six months after they moved, I asked if I could maybe move up and live with them as well. I needed to get my life in order. They were open to that, with one important ground-rule in place. No drugs. I promised them that I could do it. At that stage, I knew I needed to. I had no intention to stop smoking dope, but the speed was killing me. I could feel it.

I slowly worked up to the move, taking less-and-less speed and smoking more dope.

Three months later I made the break, moving to Rochester, about thirty minutes south of Echuca. I took up my guitar and my clothes and about two ounces of pot.

I still remember an incident about three days before I left Melbourne. I was out smoking dope at a friend's house. The friend had been sick, and I hadn't seen him in ages. He was thin and drawn with a jaundiced look about him. He had a wad of filthy bandages wrapped loosely around his neck. Each time he pulled a pipe he placed one hand flat on the front of his neck. I found it most curious so I asked him what he was doing. He didn't answer, just unwound the bandages to reveal a large band-aid stuck on the base of his throat. Mercurochrome stained the surrounding flesh a pale red. He proceeded to peel the plastic patch carefully away to reveal a raw and uneven hole in the front of his neck, dark and red and angry looking. I guess that if I shone a torch in there I'd see the back of his throat and his tonsils. He replaced the strip of plastic and spoke one word to the room in general.

'Cancer.'

He never bothered to replace the bandage as we sat and smoked in silence. He held his hand on his throat again, but it made little difference. Each time he had a pipe and breathed out, small tendrils of smoke oozed from between his fingers, twisting and curling around his shoulders and neck. It was disturbing, to say the least. I left soon after and never went back.

Rochester, here I come.

JACQUI AND THE BAND (1987-1990)

I was twenty-one when I first arrived in Rochester, and I didn't know a soul. I had brought up my guitar and amplifier, so when I wasn't looking for work, I sat at home and either read or played guitar. I brought up an ounce of marijuana from Melbourne, but no speed. I thought I'd be all right if I could get stoned, and you don't get addicted to speed – it's purely a mental thing. I did all right with it, but I was smoking a lot. I had days where I felt like going to Melbourne to score, so I figured I needed something to occupy my time. My first thought was the music. Playing guitar took me away to an easier place.

I placed an ad in the window of a music shop in Echuca for someone to jam with, and within a few days a bloke named Gary (another name that tends to reoccur in my life) gave me a call. He was a pianist and singer, and wanted me to come over for a jam. He seemed nice, if a bit hyper in his approach. His wife Julie and kids Shannon, Rebecca and Jessica all made me feel welcome, and we soon became friends.

Gary was putting together a band and was encouraging me to give it a go. I didn't think I was good enough, but had a few jams with them anyway.

💉 💉 💉

I stuck with only smoking dope at this time; trying to make the stuff I'd brought up from Melbourne last as long as possible. I started working in a residential home for the disabled, a job I heard about from Julie, who worked there as a carer.

Then, around mid-'88, I met Jacqui.

For a little extra cash, Steve – a bass player – and I agreed to play at a local birthday party. The host's nephew, Craig, was in the process of splitting up with his girlfriend, Jacqui.

I was around twenty-two, she was just turning eighteen. Short and blonde with blue eyes, Jacqui was shapely and appealing to the eye. I noticed her immediately.

Steve and I played for an hour or so, then took a break. I grabbed a drink and Jacqui came over and started talking to me straight away. Soon I was on my second drink and she was sitting on my lap. I grabbed her phone number and within a week we were dating.

Her family was a bit weird to say the least.

Jacqui was an alcoholic in denial, and her family encouraged her by drinking plenty too. I remember they even bought her a home-brew kit for her eighteenth birthday.

Her younger brother Michael, who we hung with a lot, was a chronic drug-user – smoking dope, drinking every day, and taking any other substances when the opportunity presented. There was even an old caravan set up in their backyard to party in.

They lived in Echuca, and I ended up meeting a lot of the town's drug-dealers through them.

Her older brother Chris hung with a different crowd. He was a builder and concreter by trade, and grew small drug crops in the bush near town for extra cash and to cover his own habit.

Her dad, Rob, was a former jockey and was currently working as a trainer with three racehorses. Wendy, Jacqui's Mum, who I dearly loved, was a pom with a broad Yorkshire accent. She chain-smoked and was obsessed with cleaning.

Often, Jacqui and I would come home from a night out to find her mother weeding the yard at two in the morning with the aid of the spotlights she had installed for that very purpose. Other times, when I stayed the night and slept in her brother's room because he was passed out in the van, Wendy would appear in the room at some ridiculous hour with a load of freshly-ironed clothes to put away in his wardrobe. Sometimes we would come home in the early hours of the morning to find her slumped asleep over an iron on the floor, smoke rising where it had overheated. More than once we had to douse the carpet with water to prevent it catching fire.

Jacqui and I smoked dope nearly every day during that period. I also found out she was a regular at stealing her mum's pain and anti-anxiety pills, and regularly got off her face on those. I eventually managed to get her to stop. It was a hard time for us both. I can't imagine what the withdrawals were like from the pills, as I don't know what she was taking, but it was likely a mix of opiate pain killers and benzos like Valium. We managed to get her through it, though, with a few slips on her part. I certainly respect her efforts now I know just how hard the detox from harder drugs can be.

I was really enjoying working as an attendant carer for the disabled at Campaspe House, a residential facility in Rochester. Wendy had been a career nurse before she ruined her back lifting patients, so she suggested I apply for a position at Goulburn Valley Base Hospital as a trainee enrolled nurse (EN).

Out of 1000 applicants, I was interviewed twice and then given one of the ten positions as an in-hospital trainee. I was set to move over mid-1990, for the course which ran from July 1990 until June 1991. I moved into the nurses' home there in late June.

It seemed like a dream come true: me the only guy in a big house full of girls. It was a shame I wasn't single at the time. It was also a shame I still thought of myself as useless. It's a wonder I ever managed to make a move on Jacqui. I still don't understand where I found the courage to do that.

We studied full-time for six weeks, and then worked rotating through the various wards with a study day each week. It was all paid, and the nurses' home cost about thirty dollars a week including basic coffee, tea, milk and all utilities, taken straight out of my wage each fortnight.

I really enjoyed the time living in the accommodation in Mooroopna, but Jacqui and I wanted to live together, so we started looking for private accommodation.

A couple of months later, Jacqui and I found a two-bed-room flat and she moved over from Echuca.

We settled into the routine of smoking together whenever my shifts allowed it or her drinking and smoking alone while I was at work. I made a point of never smoking before a shift, only after, so that I never went to work stoned. Lives depended on my observation and alertness. I liked to think I wasn't that irresponsible.

My parents started distancing themselves from me even more around this point. Mum didn't like Jacqui all that much, and her way of showing this was to cut off time spent with us. Sure, they'd drop over every month or so, but they never stayed long.

Wanting a career of her own, Jacqui enrolled into the local TAFE to study child-care.

Around the same time, I managed to find out she'd been abused by her uncle, so could understand to a large degree what she was trying to blank out in her memories. Now, thinking back, I have a lot more understanding of what she'd gone through and I wish I'd handled a few things differently during this time. They say hindsight is usually 20/20, and in this case it definitely was.

Jacqui's drinking got heavier up to the day I couldn't handle it anymore and kicked her out. She'd always been strong-willed and fiery, but her temper had been getting more and more erratic over the months, and we were drifting further and further apart.

It eventually got to a point where I couldn't stand it any longer. I came home for lunch one day to find her drunk and argumentative.

"What the fuck?" I said. "It's only just past midday and you're already drunk as fuck?"

"Wanna bong?" she asked, slurring her words as she pointed to a nearly-empty bowl.

"How many cans have you had?" I asked.

"A couple," she answered. There were empty stubbies and UDL cans all over the table and on the floor, so I knew she'd drank a lot more than that.

I shut the door and walked over to her, grabbing the bourbon and coke from her hand and putting it up on the bench.

"It's a bit fuckin' early, don't ya think?" I said.

"What, you're my fuckin' mother now?" she spat back at me.

"No, I'm your fucking boyfriend," I said. "Your mum'd be fine with it, but I think you drink too fucking much, Jac."

"Fuck you!" She stood unsteadily to go grab the can back.

"I'm the one that's bringing in the fuckin' money, ya drunken bitch," I yelled. "You just sit around on your arse drinking it away." I was finally fed-up with everything.

"Get fucked, cunt," she said, walking into the kitchen. I wondered what she was up to when I heard the cutlery drawer open. Next thing I knew, she was back in the lounge with a steak-knife in her hand. She lunged at me and I took a large step back. She staggered to a halt, brandishing the knife. "You ever talk to me like that again and I'll fuckin' kill ya, you prick."

"You need to get the fuck out, Jacqui," I said. "Pack your shit and get the fuck out – *now!*"

I went to slip past her, watching the knife as I did. She moved to stab me with it, but I was ready and caught hold of her forearm. I grabbed her wrist with my other hand, twisting her arm until it was up behind her back and I could safely grab the knife. She struggled, but I was too strong. I threw the knife into the kitchen and pushed her away from me.

"Pack your fucking shit now, or I swear to god I will.

Call your folks to come get you or something, but you're not staying here," I said.

She picked herself up from where she had fallen and pushed past me into the bedroom, slamming the door behind her.

I walked up and opened the door.

"What now?" she screamed at me.

"Are you gonna pack your shit or will I?"

"Fuck off and die, cunt."

I walked over to the closet and ripped it open. I grabbed her backpack and started stuffing clothes from the shelves into it. She jumped up and rushed me, swinging to hit me. I blocked her punch and pushed her away again to land on the bed. She jumped up again and rushed out of the flat, slamming the wire-door behind her. I continued to jam her clothes into her backpack and then threw it through the door into the lounge. I grabbed handfuls of clothes on hangers and took them out the front and started hanging them on the trellis that covered the front veranda. By the time I finished putting all her clothes and the backpack out the front, she still wasn't back. I went inside and rang her mother to come over and pick her up. An hour later her folks arrived.

"What's going on, Geoff?" asked Rob. He was always the calm one.

"I can't live with her any more. She drinks all the time and today she tried to stab me. You need to get her some help," I said.

"So what's she meant to do now?" said Wendy, glaring at me. "She's studying over here, so she can't drive from Echuca to school each day."

"Not my problem," I said. "She's your problem now."

Her folks piled her clothes into the car, and at that point Jacqui came home. She got in the car with her folks without a word.

I sure could have handled that a lot better, so not one of my proudest moments.

She ended up finding a room in Shepparton, near the TAFE. We never really saw much of each other after that. I've spoken to her a couple of times over the years, but we're not close. Maybe we never really were. I'm not sure just how capable I was of opening up to anyone. That may have been my problem forming relationships. I was too scared to be myself, as I truly thought I was not worthy of being loved by anyone, ever.

I was maybe nine months into my training to be a nurse at this point, but I seemed to lose direction and drive, missing days at work and finally not even sitting the final exam.

I ended up moving from Mooroopna to a house on a stone-fruit orchard about three clicks from town, and bass-player Steve moved in to share the rent. Neither of us worked, and the rent was cheap. Days and nights were spent smoking dope and playing music.

It was always in the back of my mind that I needed to get off the dope, but I ignored it.

The folks started to visit more often now that Jacqui was gone, but I don't think they approved of the lifestyle I was leading. I wasn't working, so they had no idea where my income came from. They'd drop off some groceries every fortnight, and sometimes hand me some cash. I loved them, and I guess they loved me. None of us were very demonstrative of that love. We never hugged or kissed. None of us even told the others that we loved them.

I wish I'd told them more often.

MOSES AND JULIE (1991)

When I hit twenty-four years old, another life-changing event occurred. Steve and I were at the local shop when we heard music coming from a house opposite the shop. It sounded like a guitarist playing along to Pink Floyd. We walked up the long driveway and knocked on the door. That's how we met Moses and Julie.

Mo was a throwback to the sixties. A wild-haired hippie full of angst and energy, although there was a dark side to him that was hinted at even then. I was always wary around him; always a little edgy. He was short and skinny, but there was a certain energy about him.

His wife, Julie, was newly arrived from the UK, and I always suspected her of marrying Mo to get citizenship. At twenty-eight, she was fit and attractive. She certainly looked at other guys nearly as much as they looked at her.

Mo, Steve and I formed a fast friendship, and played music. Within a week of first meeting the couple, he had shown us a homemade grow-room with about twenty plants. Mo had rigged up a spray-and-drip watering system and three large lights hooked up to a device that imitated the movement of the sun – what's called a sun circle. He'd built his own using scraps of metal and bike parts. He powered it with an old windshield-wiper motor. It was both bizarre and outrageous and so fucking clever.

Over the next month or two, he taught us how to grow dope indoors and how to set up our own room in the house we were renting. We concealed the door to the large bedroom behind wooden panelling, and grew twenty-five plants to maturity within three months of installing it. I ended up sleeping in a closet-sized space barely large enough for a single mattress, and Steve was on the couch in the lounge.

We brought in one crop in about five months. Three months to grow from cuttings, and another six weeks or so to send the plants to budding, then hanging them to dry for a fortnight. We all made a few thousand each selling them to local dealers. It was a great time, as we had all the dope we wanted and a good income after we sold everything on.

We re-invested a lot of the profits into sound and PA equipment, and formed a Pink Floyd cover band. Mo on lead guitar and vocals, me on rhythm and lead guitar, Steve on bass and Julie on keyboards. We leased a shop in Shepparton right next to the train tracks and set up a recording studio. We leased out time for locals to come in and record demo albums. Life was fine.

We decided we needed more living space, and that we should all move in together.

We'd also invested in proper equipment for growing dope, and had managed to talk a few friends into setting up their own grow-rooms. We had a deal where we'd set up the room for them, then supply the equipment and training, and we'd get the entire profit from the first crop. After that, they owned their room and carried on themselves.

We looked around for a suitable house, and we had decided we wanted a farmhouse so the electricity was part of the rent and not metred to the house. Farms use a lot of power, so our own large grow-room power drain would go unnoticed within the larger farm usage.

Eventually, we all moved into a large six-bedroom farmhouse we'd found in Shepparton South. We let the lease on the CBD shop end, and moved the recording studio into the four-car garage. Between hire fees for the PA, recording fees for local bands, and the two grow-rooms in the main house, we easily paid all our bills and set a lot of cash aside, too. We amassed over thirty thousand bucks worth of sound and PA equipment, continued performing the Pink Floyd covers at local pubs, and sold over fifty grand worth of dope in a short time.

We lived well. We always had money in our pockets and dope in our bowls.

My folks had stopped visiting completely at this point. I think Mo made them nervous. I drove over to Rochester to see them when I could, which wasn't often. Slowly, they fell out of my life.

CONFEST (1992)

onfest is a hippie/alternative gathering that takes place twice a year at Easter and Christmas/New Year. It's been a mostly annual thing since the mid-1970s, with the first one being organised by then Deputy Prime Minister Dr Jim Cairns, his private secretary Junie Morosi, and David Ditchburn. Mo told us all about it, and I really wanted to go. It's a combination of convention and festival, and it was great fun back in the day.

Easter of '92 was a real blast, sorta like how I imagine Woodstock must have been. There were hippies everywhere, tents and fire-places and open camps; it was great fun. Steve and I went, spending three days sitting around our tents and smoking heaps of dope.

Hippies and alternatives were everywhere. Naked or clothed, painted or clean(ish), there were thousands of folk there just to have a good time and connect with like-minded others. Tents and lean-to structures were all over the place, with tarps strung up over branches for some people, and fully-equipped motorhomes for others. Music, drums, market stalls, food vans, fireplaces, pathways, laughter and everything else, all blended into a massive good time.

It was a real eye-opener, especially for two guys who had severe hippie tendencies to begin with. We had an ounce of our dope with us, and shared it far and wide. This entire first Confest I'd ever attended was pretty much a blur, but one event does stick with me to this day.

We met a lot of people, including some dude who was selling morphine sulphate — a hospital-strength opiate — by the syringe-full for twenty bucks.

Each syringe held about thirty milligrams, which, to a newbie to opiates, is a large dose.

I remember sitting in my dome tent, sliding the needle into my flesh. There was a sudden rush of warmth, and pins and needles that signified it entering the system. I woke up five hours later, lying on the floor of the tent with the syringe still sticking out of my arm, the barrel jammed with blood.

I came pretty close to an overdose that day. Of course, I went straight back to the guy and bought two more fits. I made sure I was comfortable before I had the next taste.

That same year, Steve, Mo, Julie and I bought five hundred acres of land in the foothills of the Snowy Mountains – an entire valley with three permanent waterways – with drug profits. We planned to move there in a few months, and live in a commune-like set-up, growing dope and farming to meet our needs. We were pumping out as much dope in Shepparton as we could to fund this move. Growing that much dope, it was only a matter of time before something had to happen, one way or another. We had done our best to keep a low profile, but with all the other people involved, it didn't have to be our slip-up that brought us undone. We had over eight grow-rooms set up in various stages of production throughout Greater Shepparton, all capable of pumping out twenty grand's worth of dope every three months.

This could only go for so long. We just weren't smart enough to get away with it forever.

Sure enough, we got a warning in December from a friend who happened to know the local Shepparton copper. We were going to be raided, and it was due to happen in a few weeks.

We had to move to NSW a lot quicker than we'd planned.

We wouldn't be going to Confest again at the end of the year like we'd planned. Merry Christmas.

INTERSTATE (1993)

We'd already contracted to rent a vacant house in Candelo, a small town on the Sapphire Coast of New South Wales and near to the land we'd bought, so we contacted the landlord and arranged to move in early. We hired an enclosed double trailer and loaded forty-eight six-foot marijuana plants into the front half. We placed a piece of chipboard in as a false wall, hiding the plants out of sight. Then we filled the rear half with furniture.

Steve and I drove from Shepparton to Candelo, a marathon thirteen-hour drive, stopping only to eat and fill up with petrol. Every time we saw a cop car, we both near shit ourselves. With all the plants we were towing, it would be a lot of charges with definite gaol-time for us both if we were caught. We might have hidden the plants from sight behind a tonne of furniture, but as soon as someone opened that trailer the smell would hit them like a hammer. There would be no hoping the cops wouldn't notice. They'd know as soon as they opened the doors.

We did manage to get through the entire drive without getting pulled over, though, so as we approached Candelo we both breathed a sigh of relief.

When we finally hit the driveway around two in the morning it was pissing down rain. We slowed and turned into a very steep driveway that was at least six-inches deep in mud. With a heavy car and a fully-loaded trailer, we had no chance in hell of making it all the way. We tried, though, and made it about two-thirds up before we got bogged. At least we were off the road and out of sight. Pretty much safe.

By three in the morning, after numerous attempts to get the car moving but only digging ourselves in deeper despite the many boards under the rear wheels to get some grip, we started emptying the trailer by hand.

We were soaked and exhausted. We did a quick-as-possible job carrying the massive pots into the already-set-up grow-room in the main house and got the light cycle running so the plants would suffer as little as possible to the disruption of the trip, and decided to fix the rest in the morning. Finally, we had a cone or two and fell asleep in front of the fire.

We planned to live here until we finished this first crop. Then we'd sell it and get another house closer to the land we owned. Steve and Mo stayed, but I went back to Shepparton for a while. One of our mates back there, Allan, had decided he wanted to grow a big crop in a building down the back of his farm. We decided one of us would stay there and maintain the crop. I volunteered.

We set up two rooms, one in the building down the back and a smaller one inside his house. We used the small room to grow clones (cuttings) and seedlings, while the other was used for the growth and heading cycle of the current crop of plants.

I moved into a caravan out the back of his place, down near the main grow-room, spending my time playing guitar and smoking dope. I did a decent job for a month or so, making sure the crop was properly nourished and growing well. Then I found someone nearby that sold speed and I fell back into old habits. I played more and more guitar and spent less and less time caring for the plants. Eventually I let an infestation of whitefly get out of control.

When it came time to pick the crop, I pulled out four dozen spindly plants with tiny buds and loads of insects. Moses and Steve made the trip back for the drying process. They couldn't believe their eyes when I dumped the stringy things from the garbage bags onto the floor. They looked at me with disdain and disbelief as I tried to explain that the whitefly had gotten out of control before I noticed it.

They knew I wasn't stupid enough to fuck it up that much. Moses was aware I'd used speed in the past, and asked to see my arms. Ashamed, I drew up my sleeves and showed them the fresh track marks.

"Fuck, Geoff. How fuckin' stupid can you be?" Mo said.

"I fucked up, let things get out of control."

"You need to make this right, you know." Mo was angry as hell, but tried to control himself.

"I know. What can I do?"

"For starters, you can fuckin' pay for what we lost," Mo said.

I ended up parting with twelve grand I was owed from other crops. My relationship with the others was never the same after that.

🖊 🖊 🖊

Steve and I finally moved to Bega, a larger town not far away, toward the end of '93. Mo and Julie moved from Candelo onto the land we owned near Bombala, a small logging-town in the foothills of the Snowy Mountains. I spoke to my parents by phone on a few rare occasions, and they seemed okay. I loved them, but I didn't know how to say it, and neither did they. I missed them, but not enough to change. Hell, I couldn't even do that for myself.

Life seemed better for a while. I was back to only smoking dope, no more speed, and we had no shortage of cheap weed. Sooner or later we'd get busted, but with a bit of luck, it'd be later.

PART TWO

GETTING ON 1993-1999

Junk is not, like alcohol or weed, a means to increased enjoyment of life. Junk is not a kick. It is a way of life.'
Junkie ~ William S. Burroughs

CONFEST PART II (1993)

Steve and I spent Christmas of '93 at Confest on a private site a few kilometres west of Moama on the Murray River. We arrived just on dusk, and the drive in from the main road was wondrous. Five hundred metres into the farm paddocks, we were greeted at a gate by a few security volunteers. We bought our tickets and drove another 500 metres or so into the bushland main area. Another minute or two saw us into the carpark, with the main festival and camping area ahead of us. We left our sleeping bags and other gear in Steve's Valiant Charger for now, and just took our bong, cigarettes, a drink bottle and some other essentials, then wandered in to see what was what. We ended up smoking, talking, meeting new people, and falling asleep undercover at the chai tent in the market area.

The next day we grabbed the sleeping bags and ended up camping near some people we met for the rest of our stay. Days and nights of just enjoying the mellow ambiance of the festival led us to New Year's Eve.

Steve and I wanted to score an acid-trip. I asked around, and finally found a guy who was selling what he claimed was acid. He looked like a real straight, with a business shirt and slacks with leather shoes. He had a parted-on-the-right haircut and wore thick-rimmed glasses. He said he had some decent acid for sale, supposedly the real thing straight off a boat from Amsterdam. Twenty bucks each. Proper LSD, an unusual thing in the nineties. Nearly all 'trips' were blotting paper with either magic mushroom or speed-based effects.

The things he sold us were called microdots, and they certainly looked nothing like any trips I had ever seen before; tiny grey cylinders, a bout 3mm round and flat on top and bottom. More than anything they looked like the replaceable lighter flints for Zippos.

The guy made me promise not to take a whole one at once. He said we should cut one in half and share it. He said it would be a lot safer.

We got back to where we had our sleeping gear, and sat down on a log.

"So how do we do this?" Steve seemed anxious... maybe nearly as much as I was.

"I've got some sticky-tape and a razor-blade," I said. "We could wrap it in tape and then cut it in half. That way, we won't lose it."

Steve nodded and waited while I attempted to cut one of the microdots. It was harder than I thought. In the end, I gave up, worried it might shatter, and we'd lose pieces everywhere. They'd cost us twenty dollars for each one.

"Fuck this, let's just have a whole one each," I said. "How strong can it be?"

Famous last words.

For a while, maybe an hour or so after we dropped the trips, we sat around and smoked some of the hash we'd scored the day before, wondering how long it would take for anything to happen. Suddenly, I jolted. I have no other word for the feeling. It seemed like I had moved slightly sideways in space for an instant, and everything was suddenly just bizarre.

I felt like my head had swollen. My face felt all disfigured and my hands felt – and looked – thicker, fingers of plump pork sausage sticking out at odd angles from a lump of swollen meat that used to be my hand. I think I looked at my hand for at least a few minutes. God knows, it could have been hours.

I laughed, for days it seemed at the time and, like my hands, my head felt like it had gotten bigger and bigger. I remember thinking I had moved to an alien world. All the trees were odd, and they looked strange and deformed, like something out of a Dr Seuss book.

There was a layer of eerie on top of a hallucinogenic carpet ride, and moments of extreme insanity. The people were funny, the marketplace was alive and the trees were beautiful.

"Love you, tree," I said to a towering gum.

"Love you too, Geoff..." it replied.

How utterly amazing.

How wonderfully beautiful.

Scintillating colours flashed in my peripheral vision, sparkling rainbows of what seemed like ectoplasm or traces of the Northern Lights. I had a great time for the rest of that day. I didn't need any more dope. Hell, I didn't even think about scoring or smoking anything. I couldn't be any more stoned than I already was. The high felt real... it felt alive. It felt celebratory. It illuminated, and it felt exclamatory. There's no simple way to describe that trip. Not even a complex way that could ever do it justice.

"Fuck. This shit is the best trip I've ever had," Steve said, looking to me like he was melting into the ground as I focused on his face and voice.

"I don't think I've ever had real LSD before, man. All the other trips weren't like this." I think I was slurring my words, as if I'd been drinking heavily.

Sitting beside the river, we both fell silent while I contemplated the universe and all the pretty colours. God only knew what Steve was thinking. I had enough trouble keeping track of my own mind without letting my awareness seep outside to someone else's experience.

Eventually, the sun fell from the sky and evening rose up on red-rimmed wings. The heavens slowly went from blue to ochre to a beautiful deep purple, seeming like the colours were painted on the sky by madmen.

I stumbled down to the beach, where sand had been spread out for a hundred meters along the riverbank to form a swimming beach, to find candles scattered on the ground. People were lying down everywhere, and Enya was creeping carefully from hidden speakers, loud and entrancing, yet subtle and rich.

I sat down, then laid back onto the sand, floating on Enya's golden vocals and dreamlike music for what seemed like days; long and beautiful days where nothing existed but the music. Eventually I moved on, once the music stopped and the candles went out and the cold started to get to me.

The sand had cooled as the night grew deeper. It felt like it was invading my body, moving from cell to cell and freezing me a little inside as it spread. I staggered to my feet and shambled back to the marketplace, heading towards the big fire-pit to warm up. I watched the fire-twirlers ply their art in a sandy circle.

I watched streaks of fire, circles and flaring remnants of tattered cloth and fuel scattering into the night sky, embers in the stars. I fucking loved it. It blew my mind.

I moved over to lie down on the grass in the centre of the market, watching the stars as they danced just for me. I must have stayed there for the rest of the night because the next thing I can remember I was watching the sky-jewels fade from the heavens as light crept over the horizon. It bleached the black velvet above me into a dry and bone-coloured canvas before the beautiful blue I knew was coming.

As the sun rimmed over the edge of the earth, I saw a vision dancing before me. Bells tinkled and tassels dangled from a gypsy skirt all the colours of the earth and the rainbow. Humming to herself as she moved, this dervish swirled from place to place, picking up rubbish left by drugged-up hippies. I couldn't take my eyes off this blonde goddess.

I got up to help pick up some rubbish, and soon enough we were talking.

"I'm Geoff. How do you do, m'lady?"

She laughed. "Hi Geoff. I'm Ainslie and it's a pleasure to meet you."

"The pleasure is all mine." I was lost in her beauty, never normally this fluent with the opposite sex. This was so unlike me.

She was by far the most entrancing creature I had ever laid eyes upon. Blonde hair, and eyes the colour of the deepest ocean: divine ultramarine pools to draw you in if you were lucky enough to meet her gaze. Fine features, almost elfin. A beautiful, beautiful person. Ainslie was someone I fell immediately and very deeply in love with.

I spent the next couple of days in the company of this angel, and her personality was as gorgeous as she was. She was from Melbourne, out in the eastern suburbs, and that was to be my downfall. We became friends, and swapped contact details. I think I fooled myself that this time things would work out. I would get the girl and we'd be happy ever after.

TO MELBOURNE (1994)

The day I definitely decided to leave Bega came a week after we got back from Confest in January 1994.

Moses and Julie turned up at my door one morning – him in one of his moods and her apologetic for it.

"Right. It's time we started doing this properly. The last crop was shit, and we need to spend some bucks buying good quality clones." Mo's body language was angry, chest out and he was almost bouncing on his feet as though he wanted to fight me. I admit that I'd slacked off during the last crop, spending more time speeding and smoking than I'd spent caring for the plants

"How much?" I asked.

"Fifty bucks each, so fifteen hundred bucks all up. You can pay, since you cost us that much with Allan's crop." Mo glared at me.

"Fuck that," I said. 'I already paid fuckin' twelve grand for that. I covered our losses.'

"Too bad, buddy. I say you need to pay for the fuckin' clones!"

"Fuck off, Mo," I said. "You can shove that idea up your hippie fucking arse."

He tried to come at me, swinging wildly. I sidestepped just as Julie grabbed him and dragged him back out the door, which I slammed as soon as they were clear.

"You're fucking dead to me, you cunt!" screamed Mo from outside. "I'll fucking make you pay. Honour is everything. Loyalty is everything."

I never saw either of them again.

Note that two years later, I received a call from the Bega police asking if I knew where Mo was, but couldn't tell them a damn thing. Supposedly, he'd disappeared with nearly twenty grand of the commune's cash from the bank account and the land had been foreclosed by the shire for non-payment of rates. So much for Mo's honour and loyalty bullshit. He was supposed to be paying all that, yet he fucked us all over.

I packed all my things into the car, waited until my next dole cheque came in, and drove down to Melbourne. I decided I would live in the car and at friend's places until I could get into some share accommodation. I kept in touch with Ainslie, but just after I moved, I found out she had a new guy in her life. I was heartbroken and pissed off, but it was too late; I was already in Melbourne.

I arrived on a Friday in April of ninety-three, and stayed with an old friend, Maurice, and his partner Annie for a couple of days.

On the Saturday morning I bought *The Age* newspaper and started looking for share accommodation – no Internet in those days. One of the first places I looked at was where I decided I wanted to be.

Coz and Melissa were two twenty-something girls sharing a house in McHenry Street, Balaclava, right next to St Kilda on the bay. Melissa was a secretary and a fairly straight person while Coz was a punk-rocker with a hot bod and an artist running a serious heroin habit. They were both vegetarians, and I was not eating much meat at all after weeks of Confest

Not long after I arrived I caught up with a friend in Melbourne. I'd met Toothless Chris doing security at Confest. Every festival, people volunteered to keep an eye on everything through the different camping villages and the market, and we were all given walkie-talkies to stay in touch and maintain some sort of control over things. Chris was a regular volunteer. It was called security, and sometimes it was needed for an argument or people (usually local yee-haw hoons) trying to sneak in, but most often, the radios were used to let each other know about the best drugs available on site.

Most often you'd hear "Red cellophane hash for sale in the crooked tent with the runes near the main firepit in Anarchist Village" and all that sort of thing over the airwaves.

Chris wasn't just a smoker. He used speed, and that was my danger zone. I'd vowed years before to stay away from that shit, but it didn't stop me from asking for an introduction to his dealer.

Souzi lived in Richmond. She was a pleasant and attractive woman, who happened to have an influential gangster-type as an adoptive dad. Her dad Terry made and sold speed on a large scale. He was the brains and the finance behind the business, while others with the technical know-how made the drug. I think he moved a lot of product, and was very well-known in the organised crime circles of the 70s, 80s and 90s.

I got to be good friends with Souzi, and Hughey, the guy she shared the house with.

Within a month or two I had a job selling computer printers and equipment in Hawthorne. Things went smoothly for around twelve months. I smoked dope most days, and occasionally used speed (usually with Coz, as it didn't take long for us to work out we both used IV drugs). I knew Coz used heroin, but had no real interest in spending the money I could be using for speed on another drug that still scared me a little. I spent more and more time staying at Souzi's for a smoke rather than just scoring and leaving, so we became good friends.

Coz and I would go out and see bands in St Kilda, and sit at home listening to music and me smoking cones. Some nice, easy times where I actually felt comfortable to a degree.

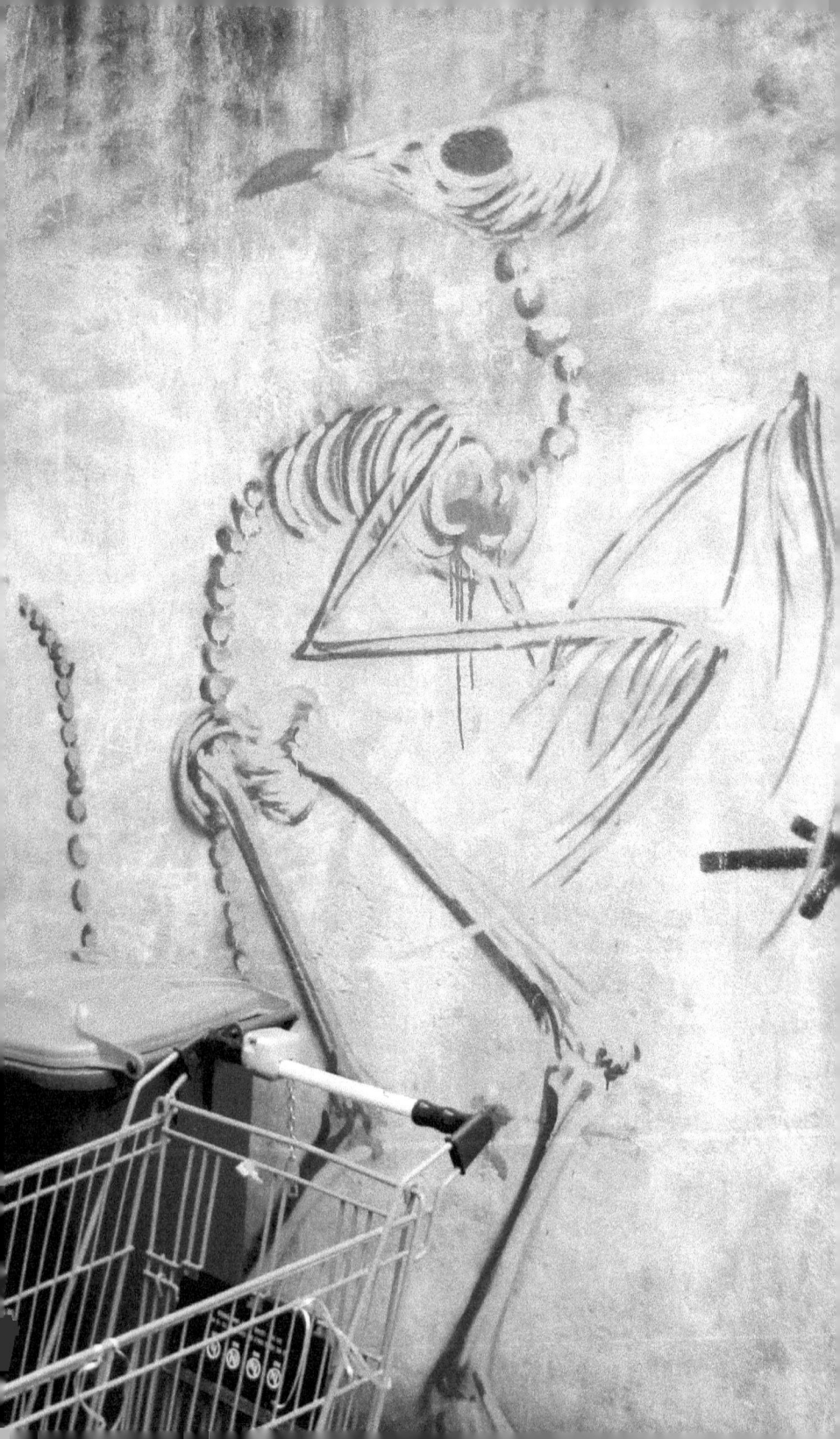

OVERDOSE (1994)

I was sitting with Mel in the lounge watching TV while Coz was in her room with a friend. I'd never liked this friend very much; she was just a typical desperate street-junkie. Coz knew her from rehab – not the best place to make friends.

Mel and I heard footsteps pounding down the hall, followed by the front door slamming shut. Curious, we both walked down and knocked on Coz's door. No answer, so we pushed it open and walked in to find her crumpled on the floor, unconscious. Next to her was a blood-stained syringe that must have fallen out of her arm as she collapsed. I reached down and checked to see if she was alive or dead. Her lips were blue and her eyes were sunken and rolled back in her head. No breath, no pulse.

"Mel, call an ambulance. Now!" I yelled as I straightened Coz out, moved the syringe out of the way, and put her flat on her back.

I don't recall consciously thinking about first aid or breathing or compressions or anything, but I managed to keep her alive until the paramedics arrived. They injected her with Narcan – a drug that totally removes the effects of opiates – but she refused to go to hospital. She went out and scored again, and then spent the rest of the night asleep. The next day she refused to talk about it. It was like it hadn't even happened. I would give CPR to two others throughout the drug years, each time keeping them alive until the professionals got there. I saw people die in front of me on at least one occasion.

One I will never forget occurred as I was going to score in the twenty-storey commission flats in Richmond a few years after I moved to Frankston later in life. As I was walking towards the front door, some poor bastard jumped from the roof, landing within fifty feet of me. I saw the body falling, thinking at first that someone had thrown a big bag of rubbish out of a window.

He hit with a splat. I kept walking, knowing there was nothing I could do for someone split open and spread twice as wide as a human body should be. I really needed a taste after that. The next day, I came past the same spot, but there was no evidence to show that someone had died there. I hunted up a couple of ice-cream sticks and made a poor effort of a cross to stick in the ground where he'd landed. Something to record what had happened.

SMACKED OUT (1994)

The first time I ever used smack was with Coz. She'd scored for herself, and out of curiosity, or maybe a subliminal need to totally fuck my life, I nagged her to share a bit with me. She didn't want to, but I kept on with it until she ended up giving me a tiny bit.

"Will that be enough to feel?" I asked.

"Fuck yeah. Any more might kill ya, or at least put you in hospital." She put twenty lines of water in the spoon with a fresh fit and sucked it up through a piece of cigarette filter.

I'd shot up plenty of times, but I felt nervous doing this. It was heroin, for fuck's sake.

I slid the needle into my arm and pressed down on the plunger. Immediately I felt a warm rush, starting in the gut and moving up my spine.

"Fuck. That's not bad," I said.

Coz looked grim. "Don't use this stuff too much, Geoff," she said. "Believe me, you don't wanna get hooked on this shit."

The nausea hit next. I ran outside and spewed all over the garden. My head was spinning and I felt real tired.

I ended up stretched out on the couch all afternoon, a bucket next to me and Pink Floyd playing on the stereo. I didn't really enjoy the nausea, but I did enjoy the numbness I felt at the same time.

Melissa moved out soon after the OD, and we rented the spare room to an office worker named Geraldine – Ger for short.

Coz and I smoked in my room or hers, and Ger didn't mind. I think she would have been a bit less tolerant with the shooting up. She drank on weekends and even smoked a joint with me a couple of times, but nothing else, nothing harder.

In September of '94, Coz started seeing a guy named Greg – a nice guy who was a dope smoker. He was good for her, a good influence. He wouldn't put up with her playing around with needles, and was wise enough to not get fooled by the typical lies and excuses.

She spent more time with him and we spent less time together as friends, and I suppose that was normal. It also meant I spent more time with Souzi, and used more speed. I was rapidly sliding back down into addiction.

In January '95 Coz and I went to the Big Day Out, a massive music festival held on Australia Day every year.

Coz and I had scored some good speed the previous day. It was hard not to use it immediately, but I managed to hold off most of the night. I eventually woke up at five thirty in the morning and couldn't wait any longer to have the shot.

As soon as I pushed down the plunger, it hit me straight away. It began with a stomach flip and a rush of energy like I'd just been plugged into a power socket. My scalp started to tingle, and it felt like my hair was standing on end. I jumped up and exploded out of my room into the hallway. Coz's door flew open and we began talking at each other a million miles per hour. She must have been already up and speeding... this was good shit!

"This is gonna be so awesome I can't wait until the band starts so what time do we have to leave to get a good car park?

"Fuck yeah hey this is good speed ain't it I reckon we should leave about seven thirty to make sure we get a park close enough to walk but still far enough to get away before too many of the crowds jam the street hey do you think we need to take any joints?" Ain't nobody got time to punctuate!

Our machinegun conversation continued until we got ready and left for the venue. Sweating and twitchy, we drove there, parked and then made our way to the entry gates.

What followed was a blur of music and movement, speed-shivers up the spine and sweat dripping from the brow.

Some great bands played that year – Dave Graney, Fur, Hole, Luscious Jackson, Magic Dirt, Spiderbait, and a young Silverchair. It was all topped off with The Offspring and Ministry. What a great day.

🪡 🪡 🪡

Around February of '95, Coz decided to move in with Greg, so her parents leased them a flat they owned. McHenry Street was officially over. The lease ran out, and Ger and I moved on.

It was a great household while it lasted, but the drug use that went on behind closed doors wasn't so great.

Smaller walk-up commission flats in Lennox St, as seen from the rear via the children's playground that sits in between Victoria St and Elizabeth St in the walkway/lane system.

SOUZI AND SLICK (1995)

I was scoring speed off Souzi on a regular basis at this point, and when she found out I was looking for a new home, I ended up moving in and renting a room from her. Hughey was moving out, so the timing was perfect. Souzi bought amphetamine straight from her father, so I got good quality straight-from-the-cook speed at a reasonable price and all the credit I could ask for. I had what I thought was a really good thing going on.

I shared with Souzi for about six months, speeding every day, playing guitar and just loafing around. Soon after moving in, she trusted me enough to handle sales while she was out. My normal routine was to wake up around 11am, have some cones with Souzi, then we'd go shopping (a daily occurrence, as Souzi loved her food fresh and we were only a couple of hundred metres from a main shopping centre in Richmond). We'd come home, cook some fresh lunch, then I'd stay home and sell drugs for her while she went and socialised with all the Richmond gangsters down at the Dover Hotel in Bridge Road, a few blocks from Waltham St, where our house was. At night, Souzi would either come home to watch TV and sell her own drugs or leave me selling all night and stay out drinking at the Dover on Bridge or the Vine Hotel on the corner of Church and Bridge.

Through Souzi, I got to know a psycho called Slick, a close associate and enforcer/debt collector for Souzi's dad Terry.

Slick was a textbook speed-freak, full of paranoia and full of his own ego – a dangerous combination. Always armed with a pistol and large amounts of speed, Slick was an unstable and dangerous person.

Speed psychosis is an ever-looming threat when you use amphetamines. It can manifest in a variety of different symptoms, but there are a few that seem universal: hallucinations, paranoia and, worst of all, rarely-controlled violent behaviour. Combine these and you've got a very volatile situation.

One day we got the news that the cops had executed a search warrant on the house Terry used as a speed lab. They'd arrested the cook, and the cops were now after Terry. He took off and hid out in Queensland until he felt safe enough to come back, but meanwhile Slick was still around and had nowhere to score. I'd kept in touch with Oz, who was now living in Melton. Slick asked me to ring him and arrange a deal.

Slick used large amounts of speed. He usually shovelled a teaspoonful of gear into his mouth every three or four hours, which is a horrendous amount of speed for anyone. Slick was out of control.

He came around to Souzi's place one day and asked if I could get onto an ounce for him, that he'd give me a gram if I did him the favour. I told him I'd try, so he left to look elsewhere while I called Oz. About an hour later, I called him back.

"Hey Slick, it's all good, man. Eight hundred bucks and it's yours."

"When can we get it?"

"Now. By the time we get out to his place, it'll be there waiting."

Getting in his old ute, we drove to Melton in anticipation of the score – Slick because he was desperate for some gear after days with nothing and me just hanging for a taste, as usual.

We got close to Oz's place, and I told him to park and wait over to the side of the road.

"I'll need the cash, man," I said.

Slick glared at me. "Can't I come in with ya? I wanna meet the guy anyway."

"Not gonna happen, Slick. You know how it works. I'll ask him this time if I can bring you in next time. Okay?"

He mumbled something under his breath and handed me eight hundred in fifty-dollar notes.

He seemed irritated and edgy that I wouldn't let him come in with me, but that was drug protocol; you never take someone to meet a dealer unless the whole thing was organised in advance. As far as I was concerned, it would never happen with these two. I just didn't trust Slick enough to vouch for him. It was as simple as that.

I'd parked around the corner so he couldn't see where I was going, and as I walked I checked behind to see if he was spying on me.

I reached Oz's house and rang the doorbell. Belinda answered and ushered me inside.

"Hi Bee. How's things?" I asked.

"All good, thanks Geoff. Darren's in the lounge. Go on through."

I went in and found Oz sitting on the couch, guitar in hand and a KISS concert on the VCR and through the stereo as he played along with it.

"Hi, mate. How's it going?" I sat down next to him and pulled out the cash. "How'd you go with the ounce?"

"Yeah, mate. No worries." He paused the video, placed the guitar on its stand and reached behind some books on a shelf next to him.

"Here you go." He handed me a plastic zip-lock baggie half full of white powder.

"Thanks, mate." I handed him the cash and he stuffed it away in a pocket without counting it. He had good reason to trust me: I'd never ripped him off.

We talked a bit more then I made my exit.

I walked back and got in the car, handing the baggie to Slick. He opened it and jammed an old spoon in, scooping out a heap of speed and shoving it into his mouth.

We drove back, and by the time we hit Footscray, he wouldn't shut up.

He gave me about a gram of the drug, and we were both happy.

I scored three more times for him before he was able to source his own once more and thought nothing more of it. I should have known better.

CAROLYN (1995)

Souzi and her friend Carolyn, who I thought was pretty cute and liked a lot, were out partying during the Moomba festival. I stayed home to sell speed for Souzi as usual and practise guitar.

Although speeding, I had been up for three days straight already, so I managed to get to sleep around one am, once the customers had stopped dropping in.

The sound of the bedroom door opening woke me up about three in the morning.

"Hey Geoff... you awake?" It was Carolyn.

"I am now," I said.

"We just got back from Moomba, and Souzi doesn't remember where she put the spare doona. It's late and I'm too drunk to go home... do you mind if I climb in with you?"

"Er... yeah, no worries," I said.

She slipped out of her jeans, leaving a singlet and g-string on as she slid in next to me. I was nervous as hell. I liked her a lot, and I always had a terrible record with girls and women I liked. I seemed to have never gained the ability to make the basic human connection that moved to a true relationship. Even the ones I'd had seemed somehow lacking. I just had no ability to truly open myself to others to the extent required for a meaningful, deep connection. I remember praying for a second, consciously praying to the universe, this would move forward in a more normal way.

We lay there for a few minutes, snuggled together. Eventually she broke the silence.

"So, how do you feel about casual sex?" she asked.

"Sounds good to me."

"Do you have any condoms?" she asked. I didn't, but

there was a Coles about 300 metres away, so I think I broke the land-speed record getting there and back before the dream vanished and I was left alone once more.

I actually nearly cried out with joy to find her there waiting for me.

I slid back into bed. She pulled her singlet off, revealing perfect tits and a nice tight body. What followed lasted all night.

We fucked a couple more times over the next few weeks. Soon enough, we settled into some sort of a weird, non-committed relationship, at least as far as she was concerned.

Carolyn usually worked as a stripper, but not currently. She had two kids – Naomi, who was seven, and Julian, who was four. They both had different fathers. Naomi's dad was an addict named George, a long-time friend of Souzi's. I'd known him for years, and liked him. Julian's dad was a different story – he was a violent bastard named David. He used to bash Carolyn all the time. She ended up calling the Department of Human Services for help, but all they did was take the kids away and place them with Carolyn's mother.

Around this time, Slick began to treat me differently, as though he held a simmering anger towards me for something. I had no idea what his problem was, but it all came to a head one Friday night in June of '95 at Souzi's house.

I felt the room tension change as he walked down the hall and into the lounge. I felt a kind of buzz in the nerves of my fingertips and on the back of my neck. My scalp tingled and it felt like my hair was standing on end. I felt nervy and on edge, so it wasn't really a surprise when Slick spoke.

"You fucking cunt. Ya fucking ripped me!"

I was sitting in the lounge room with Souzi, we had just had a cone and Slick was standing in the kitchen doorway. He stared at me while he said this.

I edged forward in my chair, getting my feet under me. "What the fuck are ya talking about?" I asked.

"I'm talking 'bout when ya scored for me, how you taxed it before ya got back to the car." He shuffled his feet a little and glanced down at the floor before looking back at me. I got to my feet carefully, so as not to spook him. "What the fuck are you talking about, Slick?" I said. "Of course I fucking didn't. Apart from the fact I'm not a fucking thief and the fact you were going to give me some anyway, I had no fucking chance to do that. It was the middle of the fucking day on a street full of houses. You think I'm stupid enough to pull out an ounce of fucking speed and risk someone seeing and calling the cops on us?"

He's a big guy, tall and lanky, and he's strong and violent to boot, so the whole thing worried me. Speed freaks can be volatile at the best of times. As I stood up in case he went nuts, he pulled a pistol out of his pocket. "Ya fucking thieving dog, I should fucking knock ya right now!"

At the sight of a gun, I ran to the front door as fast as I could. I don't know what he did 'cause I was too busy trying to move left to right in the hall as I bolted. I had no weapon, he had a gun and I knew he was bat-shit crazy enough to shoot me. I just had no idea why.

I made it out of the front door without any bullets hitting me. I don't know if he did pull the trigger or if Souzi had calmed him down or what, but I sure as hell wasn't sticking around to give him a chance to put a bullet in me.

Once I was sure Slick hadn't followed me down the street, I walked to a mate's place about five blocks away. I ended up staying there with Woody for a week, and then I found out he needed a new housemate anyway, so I officially moved in.

No matter how much Souzi wanted me as a housemate, Slick was too unpredictable. I found out later she ended up calming him down and calling Terry, who spoke to Slick and told him to stop being so fucking stupid. He also reminded Souzi that Slick was pretty fucked-up lately, and it might be best if I moved on.

I only ever saw Slick once more, and that was at Woody's house a week later. I answered the door one night to find him standing there in the rain, a sheepish look on his face. He asked if we could talk somewhere private, so I led him out the backyard, heart hammering at the thought of getting shot.

"What the fuck is it this time, Slick?" I tried to steady my breathing and not show how freaked I was.

"I just thought I'd drop over and see ya. Terry asked me to. Souzi likes ya, so Terry likes ya."

"And...?" I said, sweat starting to form on my brow.

He slipped the same small revolver out from behind him, most likely tucked in his jeans in the small of his back. He watched me for a reaction. He got none.

He laughed and put it away in his coat pocket.

"I might have been a bit out of line last time I saw ya," he said. "Sorry 'bout that, Geoff."

I breathed a soft sigh of relief. "No worries, Slick. People do that to me all the time." I laughed, a little bit more settled now he seemed to have no immediate plans to shoot me.

He left quickly, out of a misguided sense of shame, I suppose. My guess would be it wasn't shame at his actions, but shame at being told to apologise for them.

PEP AND NOEL

As usual, I had trouble connecting with people, so I didn't stay long at Woody's place. Plus, even though Woody like to smoke dope, he wasn't into IV drugs, and didn't like Carolyn dropping around either. A month or so later, around August of '95, I moved into a house in Coburg with a couple I knew through Coz. Pep was a small, dynamic beauty – a real looker. She was also a working girl, a prostitute. Noel, her boyfriend, was a complete psychopath.

He'd grown up around Cairns, where my uncles lived. It seems he'd known and respected my cousins back in the day in Queensland, and this was enough to supposedly convince him that I was all right. He'd left Queensland after getting involved in a murder up there.

While I was living there, Julian's dad – David – decided that he wanted me hurt for, as he saw it, 'taking Carolyn off him'. He somehow managed to arrange to have me bashed by a bikie club from Queensland.

One morning, Noel knocked on my bedroom door.

"Geoff. There's some bikers coming into town for you," he said.

"Wha...?" I asked, still half asleep.

"There's a fuckin' bike club lookin' for ya."

"What're you fuckin' on about?"

"Doc called to let me know," he said. Noel hung around the Hells Angels, and through him Souzi and I had managed to meet some of them and do some business.

"I'll talk to the boys. Find out what's goin' on," Noel said.

Within a day, word came back that David actually had arranged to have me bashed, but the other club had been warned off by the Angels. No other club was welcome to come into their territory to cause trouble.

I didn't hear any more about it. Sometimes it's nice to have friends in low places.

Not long after this, I moved to a small house down near Phillip Island with Noel and Pep.

Carolyn had called off our relationship to try and make it work one last time with David, for the sake of Julian. I never understood how going back into an abusive relationship was good for anyone, but logic rarely comes into these sorts of decisions. I pretty much know she was at least as damaged as I was by life, and now I can't blame her for any of the silly decisions either of us made over the years. This new thing with the old boyfriend lasted about three weeks, until he bashed her again. After that, we took up where we'd left off.

I was twenty-eight and she was thirty.

About the same time, I reconnected with my parents when I decided I needed to give them a call.

"Hi Mum," I said, when she answered the phone.

"Geoff?" she asked, likely surprised to have me call up out of the blue like this.

"Yeah, it's me," I answered.

"Well, I guess it's nice to hear from you after all this time. We've been worried, and the phone number you used to have is not working... Where have you been?"

"Around," I said. "I'm back in Melbourne, and it looks like I'll be staying down here for a while."

"Can you come up for a visit?" she asked. "We'd like to see you."

"I don't have transport, and I'm doing a lot of hours with a nursing agency," I lied.

"Well, when you get the chance, it'd be good if you could come over and see us," she said.

"Yeah, I'll try," I said. "Um... the reason I called is to ask if you guys could loan me some money. I have to get to work by train, and I don't have the cash for fares until I get paid next week."

"I suppose so," she said. "How much do you need?"

"A hundred bucks should see me through with fares, food and somewhere to stay," I answered.

"I'll put in a bit extra," she said. "You'll need new clothes for work."

"I guess I will," I said.

"I'll need your bank numbers," she said.

I gave her the account details, broke off the call and waited an hour until some money went into the bank. I went straight to Souzi's and scored some speed.

Carolyn and I got back together after she left David again. She was living at her Mum's place in the south eastern suburbs of Melbourne, with her kids in foster-care while she waited for the housing commission to give her access to cheap rental. The house turned up six weeks later, in late November. It was in Frankston North, a place known as The Pines, a broken-down Housing Commission area. Full of drugs and dysfunctional families, it was a dangerous place to live.

THE PINES (1996)

I t seemed The Pines was so fucked up that even Carolyn didn't feel safe living there alone with the kids, so she asked if I wanted to move in.

We lived within a hundred metres of a row of shops where people gathered of a night. In the mornings you'd usually find blood, beer bottles and syringes scattered around the parking area in front of the shops. Sometimes you would find teeth as well.

Carolyn was a heroin user but she wasn't running a habit when I moved in. The potential was there, though, and soon enough we found out that we could get hold of smack in Frankston, barely two kilometres away. Whenever we scored, Carolyn had most of the gear as she already had a tolerance. I was still a newbie to smack. No tolerance; no habit. I needed a lot less to get off than she did, and if we shared the drugs equally, she would barely feel it and I'd likely OD. I probably had an eighth of whatever we scored, but it was still enough to make me spew every time I had it. I curled over the toilet bowl too many times to count, and the kids were getting sick of me pulling over to puke on the side of the road whenever we went out.

There were dealers on the street near the Frankston train station every day from sunrise till well after dark. It was easy to score, and we had our choice of dealers every time we went down there. I didn't like the idea of scoring off the street, having to look for people and wait for them to show up, so we made sure to get a few phone numbers from people who also dealt from their homes.

Our next-door neighbours were druggies as well. Soon enough, we'd get to know them, and through them we'd meet all the junkies and smack dealers in the area.

Health and Community Services had placed the kids in foster care while Carolyn waited for a house, mostly due to David's violence. Once she had a place, the court gave her custody again. Having no children of my own, I soon grew to love them both very much.

Julian was five years by now, and a real little bugger. He always pushed the boundaries of acceptable behaviour, mostly to get attention. Naomi was eight and a little sweetheart; always wanting to help with the housework and cooking, always ready to lend a hand.

I was throwing up outside the back door one day when the neighbour stuck his head over the fence and asked if we were junkies. I've never liked that term.

"Dunno what you're talking about, man. I'm just sick."

"Yeah, right. Looking at your arms, I'd say that ya get as sick as I did when I first started using smack." He looked at me and shook his head, handlebar moustache flicking up as he smiled.

It seemed useless to deny it any further after he showed me the track-marks on his own arms.

Brendon was a daggy-looking guy sporting an overgrown mullet with a sideburn-moustache combination.

He was with a skinny, scraggy woman called Charlene. They had three kids: Kara, eight, Michelle, who was eleven, and Cody, who was about three. The two girls used to come and play with Carolyn's [*our*] kids all the time. Next-door's brood never had clean clothes, rarely wore shoes – even in winter – and would always tell us they wished that we were their parents. Considering our situation, it made me wonder just how fucked-up their place was.

GAINING A HABIT (1996)

Eventually, using smack a few times a week became using smack daily. We smoked dope constantly, used speed when we felt like it, but I loved the numbness brought on by Heroin. It was the great equalizer when it came to emotions. It eradicated everything, without bias. It took away all the memories of every painful thing, and covered them with the fog of the opium dreamer. There were definitely downsides to it. It was bloody expensive, and the vomiting continued, but seemed to be settling to less than an hour before I could safely sit on the couch and just enjoy the blankness. There were days we couldn't get the cash to score, and after a week or so, Carolyn started to suffer withdrawals, whereas I hadn't been using long enough to have a habit. I didn't like seeing her so uncomfortable, though, so we moved more and more of our income over to smack. That made it hard to keep up with the other bills, but we did what we could.

I'm not proud to say a number of times I rang the folks for money, giving them a sob story about fines I needed to pay or not having money to eat or smashing the car and needing to pay for repairs. Then the next day I'd call and say the person I'd hit wanted their car fixed or they were going to sue me or have me charged by the coppers. I did some shameful things to the people who loved me the most. That's what junkies do.

Even with this extra income, on top of Carolyn's pension and my unemployment payments, the cost of the smack was starting to show in our lifestyle.

We were getting what was called 'alkaline' smack back then. It was a dirty brown rather than the pure white colour of the better China White, and needed a drop or two of vinegar or lemon juice added so it dissolved in the spoon. It also had to be heated, rather than instantly dissolving like the purer stuff. It wasn't as bad as the black tar heroin most common in the US, but it did have a higher percentage of unprocessed opium in it rather than being almost pure H.

It made me sick both physically and emotionally, which is weird when it covers emotions. Here I was, using heroin, something I never thought I'd do. I was one-step removed from the guilt of being fucked-up all the time, but it also made me feel better mentally and emotionally. Whenever I was stoned, I forgot all about my problems. I forgot about my childhood and how it made me feel. The empty black hole, the broken thing deep inside me was filled for a moment, or at least covered up enough the darkness would edge away. I liked that lack of feeling. I almost loved it. There was no way I was going without it.

Every day became the same. Wake up, score if we had cash or try to get cash if we were broke. Usually by begging, borrowing or stealing.

We found reliable dealers in Frankston when we could, and we went to Springvale or Richmond when we had to. Cops were everywhere in the mid-90s, trying to slow down the drug-dealing in the suburbs where street smack lived, and they busted street dealers more and more often. Teams of coppers with sniffer dogs inundated the drug suburbs, searching addicts and dealers alike. This slowed down a lot of the public heroin trade, especially in Richmond, forcing desperate junkies to hang around the commission flats, hoping to find someone scoring through a private contact that would let them tag along for the transaction. The whole scene was a real mess for a while, with established distribution centres blown wide open and everyone trying to start up new routines. It caused havoc on the streets, and caused more crime as drug prices soared because of the shortage. Addicts would willingly pay nearly twice the previous prices to stop going into withdrawal. Nothing else mattered once the cold sweats and the restless legs kicked in. The cops gloated over multiple arrests every week, but the people living in the areas knew it was only making things worse. The media loved it, though.

ROUTINE (1996)

The scruffy guy had no idea what was about to happen. I'd just gotten off the bus near Frankston train station when I saw it go down. He was standing there, looking around as if waiting for someone. Suddenly there were guys all around him, badges hanging from chains around their necks. They moved in fast. One of them grabbed him by the arm and swung him around. Another grabbed his throat. They both threw him to the ground and wrenched his arms behind him so that he could be 'cuffed. The cops held him down and searched him, finding what looked like a baggie full of balloon-wrapped deals of smack. A divvy-van pulled up and he was thrown in the back and carted away.

Nearly every day, the cops arrested someone for selling smack on the streets. The cops were really trying to clean up the drug trade. There were rumours they'd set up surveillance cameras in the old Commonwealth Bank building. It was opposite the station and had a great view of the main drug sales spots.

People soon learnt to go around the corner into the car park near Cash Converters or down the mall to buy and sell their drugs. The rate of arrests dropped, the media and the police moved onto something else. Within about a month, it all went back to business as usual.

After I watched the dealer get arrested, I walked down Station Street, toward the shopping mall, where I kept an eye out for anyone I knew.

I walked past the shops, watching for anyone from the local scene, as well as watching out for potential undercover cops. It was a Friday, so there was a fair crowd. It was easier for me to blend in, although I don't doubt that my face was known to the cops.

I lifted my sunglasses, so I could make eye-contact once I saw someone I knew.

I got as far as the pawn shop on the corner of Clyde St and spotted Tim. He was sitting in Clyde St, watching out for people who might want to score.

I walked over. "Hi mate. Anything?"

"Yeah. How many you want?" he asked.

"Three, man." Each cap was forty bucks, but most dealers sold three for a hundred.

He grunted something in response and struggled to his feet. He walked toward the mall, spitting the deals into his hand. I followed at a distance designed to make sure people didn't realise we were together. I pulled two fifties from my pocket and got ready to pass them. He slowed down, and as I caught up, he grabbed the cash from me and palmed me three small parcels tied up in water-balloons. I wiped them carefully on my shirt and popped them into my own mouth.

If the cops tried to grab me, I'd swallow them. Looking around, there didn't seem to be anyone overly interested in me, so I left and walked back toward the station to catch a bus home.

I found that most dealers prefer a quick exchange of cash and drugs in the middle of the crowd, which is why most smack-zones are also main shopping streets. Too much movement, people all around, makes it harder for surveillance cameras to catch people in the act, and makes the subtle transaction harder to spot. There are guys who try to evade 'selling' charges by keeping a lump of gear and chopping a bit off for each sale as they go. They can try to claim it's all for personal use, but this also makes it harder to hide the gear or dump it if the cops grab them.

VIOLENCE (1996-97)

Around November of '96, Julian's father, David, decided he wanted to have Julian for Christmas. It seemed to me more like the last ditch effort of a man desperate to get back with Carolyn. David had settled in Queensland with a new girlfriend. He had found a job cleaning schools for cash, so he could avoid the massive child-support debt he owed. Even so, he wanted back with Carolyn, and we both knew what his motives were for wanting to see Julian.

The holiday went as planned, and David justified our suspicions by suggesting that Carolyn go up for a second week, to stay at a motel he had 'arranged' for her. Needless to say, that didn't happen. She'd finally broken that link, gotten him out of her mind and moved on.

Afterwards we found out David had lived up to his character by treating Julian badly while showering presents on his girlfriend's kids for Christmas. Julian wasn't even allowed to play the Playstation the other kids got as a present.

We picked Julian up from the airport without incident on the thirtieth of December, but there was an incident on the way home.

A studious-looking twenty-something in a small Japanese car cut us off quite badly on the Tullamarine Freeway going back towards Melbourne. I had to brake hard to avoid hitting the back of his car, and was pissed at his careless driving. I moved the car up next to him. "You fucking dog," I screamed.

He and his girlfriend both laughed hysterically and gave me the finger. I followed them to the first set of traffic lights, and got out of the car to have words with them. At the same time, Carolyn got out and followed me.

As I reached the front doors, I heard the click of the central-locking as I made eye contact with the driver. They started laughing, giving me the finger again.

Fuckers think they're so clever? I'll show 'em clever.

I reached over and grabbed his driver-side wiper-blade, tore it off and threw it to the ground. At that point, Carolyn began pounding on the passenger door. I stepped back and push-kicked his side mirror, snapping that off and sending it skittering along the road.

He put his car in reverse and took off backwards – slamming into our car. It was enough to crack open my grill and crush the bonnet.

He shifted into drive and screeched towards me, trying to run me down. Carolyn ran back to our car screaming for Julian. He was in the back seat, and I was worried he may have been injured. I went to run back to the car as well, but the moron came too close, forcing me to jump sideways into the traffic. A large truck just missed me. I felt the wind as it passed, doing at least eighty clicks through what was now a green light, just turning amber.

The guy came to a stop as the lights changed to red again. I ran to his car, enraged beyond words. Carolyn was screaming that Julian was bleeding. I remember slamming my fist into the driver's-side window and smashing through the glass. I didn't feel my fist connect with his temple and I didn't feel the glass punch into the side of his head, slicing it open.

Slamming his car into drive, he screeched away through the red light. I managed to pull my arm from the window just in time to avoid some nasty cuts. My hand was covered in shattered glass and blood, only a little of it mine.

We drove home, our car overheating from the damage. I washed and bandaged my hand and fumed about the arsehole that had done this. Julian had a large cut on his forehead from the impact where he's slammed forward and hit the front seat. There was blood everywhere and he was close to hysterical over the whole thing. I've definitely had better days.

It came to a head two days later when the cops knocked on the door to charge me with assault and criminal damage. Seems the arsehole had taken my numberplate and gone to the cops with his own version of the story where was purely the victim rather than nearly as complicit as myself. They showed me a photo taken at the time of his complaint and it looked like he'd been mangled. Blood all over his face and his hair soaked in it, bandages soaked in blood and swollen forehead. I ended up in Prahran court a few weeks later. He lied to the magistrate about what had happened, and even though I put forward my side of what happened, in the end I was found guilty, placed on a Good Behaviour Bond and fined a thousand bucks. I now see I elected to escalate the situation more than I should have.

About two months later, I used a contact in the police to find out the guy's address from the number plates I'd memorised. He lived in Richmond, so I ventured over there late one night.

I parked about a block away. I grabbed a bottle of brake fluid I'd bought for the occasion and walked up to the block of flats where he lived. Sure enough, his car was parked there. He'd had the back repaired. I opened the bottle of brake fluid and poured it all over the roof. It dripped down the sides and began oozing down the windscreen. I poured what was left in the bottle all over the bonnet and the boot and walked away, taking the empty bottle with me. He'd find his car in the morning, paint-job ruined.

HABIT BORN (1997)

It was five in the morning, and I was suddenly wide-awake. I felt cold yet sweaty, my legs were sore, and I had the strangest tingling feeling all over. Like millions of bugs were crawling over my skin. I tried to go back to sleep, but there was zero chance of that. I lay there, trying to get comfortable but it only got worse and worse.

"What the fuck, Geoff?" mumbled Carolyn.

"Fucked if I know," I said. "I think I'm coming down with something."

"What is it?" she asked.

I described the different things I was feeling. She just looked at me.

"I think you're hanging out," she said. "I think it's finally caught up to you. All this scoring. All this using. I did warn you, y'know." She sighed, and rolled over to rub my chest.

"Don't stress too much. The first time is actually pretty tame."

It seemed I had reached the level of addict. Achievement unlocked.

I lay there while Carolyn tried to go back to sleep. I had cold sweats and hot flushes at the same time. I needed to shit really badly all the time, but when I got up to go to the dunny, nothing came out except a vile-smelling, green-brown fluid. I went to the lounge room and put on a fan, but that felt weird on my skin so I turned it off again. Sweat covered every inch of my body and I felt like crap.

We needed to score. I knew how Carolyn had felt all those times she complained about hanging for a taste. I'd had no idea it would be this bad. Now I could see why it was so important to her that we get on as quickly as possible.

Throughout my time as a junkie, I would find out that, as time went on, the symptoms got worse. Day one of hanging was a breeze compared to days three and four. Also, the bigger the habit, the harder the withdrawals.

Sunday a month or so later we'd gone to visit Honey and Simmo, friends of Carolyn's who lived in Altona. It wasn't well-planned, as I still hadn't really worked out a rhythm for scoring and using wisely to make sure we got through the night. It was a bad time to visit anyone, as we had no money, and it was close to the end of our Social Security pay fortnight. We were already slightly sick when we arrived on the Saturday. We thought we'd be okay until the Sunday, when I could go sell a few books at the local market.

By the time we went to bed, the sweats had started. We shared a single bunk bed while Julian and Naomi shared the top. We suffered there all night, shivering and cramping and sweating and shaking. I had to race to the toilet at least ten times to throw-up or take a crap.

Around 5am, I was staring at the underside of the bunk above us, trying to suffer in silence so we didn't disturb the kids too much. That was the hardest part, I think. Cramps, nausea, restless legs and cold-sweats combined to take me to hell for the night. I remember what I can best describe as the feeling of electric fleas crawling all over, just under the surface of the skin. Fleas that, when they bit, gave a shock. Even their feet crinkled the skin in a horrendous way. It was a living hell, and the worst part was I couldn't get to sleep to escape it. It seemed forever before the sun came up so we could get the fuck out of there and try to score.

We went to start the car as soon as we'd packed and woken up Honey and Simmo to say goodbye, but the damn battery was flat. What a time for this to happen. I went and asked Honey and Simmo to give us a hand.

It took three of us to push-start the car. Driving back over the Westgate Bridge was hell; sweat and shivers nearly causing me to lose focus a few times before I noticed I was maybe drifting a little close to the next lane. Purely focused on how to score. Finally, we made it to Richmond. While Carolyn took the kids to a nearby playground, I rang Mum.

"Hi Mum."

"What's happened?" she asked. "What do you want now?"

"We had a bit of trouble coming home just now from a friends place," I said. "The battery was flat, so we managed to get it going, but it just won't charge up. I think the alternator's done for."

"And?" she said. "Get it fixed."

"I would, if I had the money."

"Aren't you working? What are you doing with all your money?"

"Paying bills," I said. "Trying to feed the kids and get all their school clothes and stuff."

"If I give you some money, will you get the car fixed?" asked Mum.

"Yeah. We've got a guy lined up today. He said he'd do it cheap for us, with a reconditioned part, but I need to get it done now so I can go to work later on. I have an arvo shift," I lied.

She deposited two hundred bucks into a TAB betting account for me and we drove to Richmond to score.

It's hard scoring and shooting up with the kids around, so Carolyn waited with them in a playground near the car park while I met the dealer, mulled up and injected my share.

As soon as I slid that needle into my arm, my gut loosened, and ten seconds later I felt almost human again. I walked back to the playground with Carolyn's share, carefully passed her a tissue with her share already mixed into a syringe, and stayed with the kids while she took the keys and went to have her hit in the car. We were fine again, at least until it wore off later that afternoon, but by then I'd dropped Carolyn and the kids off at home and gone on a book-stealing spree to get enough money to score again.

A week later, on the Saturday, Mum called to say that my dad had had a heart-attack and died. I clutched the phone, unable to respond for a second, and felt my world turn upside-down. I'd never been as close as I felt I should have been to my parents, but they had always done the best I could for me, and I loved them both very much.

Carolyn and I dropped the kids off at her Mum's and drove straight up to Bendigo. Mum and Dad had been selling antiques at a weekend market when he collapsed out behind one of the big sheds at the market site.

We arrived in Bendigo, at the market, to find a crowd gathered around Mum, helping her by packing up the stock on the table of the stall they had every week. She looked devastated.

We rushed over and I sat down beside her, holding her hand as the tears flowed from us both.

"What happened," I asked.

"Dad's dead," she said. She was grey, looked in shock, and it broke my heart to see her that way.

I couldn't get a lot of sense out of her, she was so upset. I left Carolyn to comfort her for just a second and went to talk to the market organiser, who was standing nearby. She told me what had happened.

It seems Dad had gone to sit in the car, parked behind the main shed, because he was feeling sick.

He'd been out there on his own, and must have felt the attack coming on. He'd gotten out of the car, but had collapsed by the open door. Someone had found him and called an ambulance, but it was too late. He was dead, and couldn't be revived.

Carolyn and I took Mum home to Rochester. I quickly drove back to Melbourne that afternoon and scored a couple of grams of smack so we could stay with Mum and help with getting everything organised.

The next day, we drove down to Bendigo to view the body. We arrived at the hospital and went to the reception desk.

"Hi. My name's Geoff Brown. We're here about my dad. He died yesterday, out at Guildea Lane Market," I said. I felt numb.

The receptionist directed us to the morgue.

"Are you sure you're okay with this, Mum?" I asked, as we walked down the corridor.

"I need to see him," she said. I held Carolyn's hand, and held onto Mum's arm to share some strength. Mum stumbled a little, and I held her up.

Finally, we reached the morgue. A nurse took us to a small waiting area. A few minutes later, she came back and led us through to a viewing room.

"The deceased may look different to how you remember them," she said. "Don't be surprised by this."

A set of double doors opened and a trolley was wheeled in; on top, a body was laid out, covered by a sheet. Mum sagged against me and Carolyn gripped my hand. An attendant pulled back the sheet to reveal a body, pale and drawn. He was skinnier than I thought, and the hair was all wrong, too.

"That's not my dad," I said.

"People always look different when they have passed on," replied the nurse.

"No," I said. "That is *not* my father. My dad didn't have any tattoos, and that guy has one on his arm." I could see the little edges of a tattoo rising up from the guy's arm.

They had made a big mistake. It seems Brown was a common name in the morgue that day. Soon enough, I'd convinced them enough to check, and they brought in the right body.

Mum collapsed to the floor and I felt dizzy and light headed. A nurse helped Mum to a chair back in the waiting area, and Carolyn and I went to join her. The rest was a blur. We ended up downstairs at a coffee-shop, sitting quietly. Our drinks went cold and untouched in front of us. No-one said anything. I had no idea what to say. I just held my mum's hand and we sat in silence.

When we finally left the hospital, we drove over to the funeral home and made the rest of the arrangements. Afterward, we went back to Rochester, where Carolyn and I had a big taste of smack so I could dull the pain. Plus, the withdrawals were starting.

The next two days I spent as stoned as I could get. I had to go back to Melbourne the day before the funeral to score again. I borrowed the money from Mum. I told her I needed to pay some bills and I didn't have the money. She lent me five hundred, so I scored another gram of gear.

Finally, the day of the service arrived. We were all up early to get ready.

I dragged myself out of the single bed Carolyn and I were sharing. "I'll make up a taste if you want to put the kettle on for a coffee," I said to her.

"Fine. I'll be back in a sec," she said.

She shut the door behind her as I grabbed the little leather purse we kept the gear in. I grabbed a spoon from the desk and put a big rock in it. I grabbed a glass of water left from last night's taste and opened two new syringes from the purse. I'd measured out half a mill of water and mixed the gear into it by the time she returned with two cups of coffee.

"Your mum's up," she said as she put the cups down on the desk.

We had the smack, felt better, [*numb*], showered and drove to Bendigo for the funeral.

We arrived at the Neangar Memorial Park Crematorium just before ten. There were a few friends and relatives already gathered outside the small chapel. I was stoned enough to feel very little, but I still felt a vague sense of loss. Dad had always been disappointed in me. He never said so, but I always saw it in his eyes. At least, I thought I did. Carolyn held onto me, and I helped Mum inside and sat her down.

The reverend from the church next door to my parent's house in Rochester had volunteered to perform the service. He came over to talk to us.

"How are you, Lynette?" he asked.

"I'm fine, Peter," Mum said.

"That's good," he replied. He looked over to Carolyn and me. "Are you okay, Geoff?"

"I'm fine, too," I said. I think I was lying, but I was so stoned I wasn't sure.

He tried to console us before moving off to welcome the other attendees.

Steve from Bega was there. He'd been in Echuca visiting his parents, and must have seen the death notice. He came over to see us.

"Hey, Geoff. Sorry to hear about your dad," he said. "Hi Mrs Brown. I'm so sorry."

I introduced him to Carolyn, and we sat and made small talk. All the other relatives and friends came and mouthed empty platitudes, and it became a blur. Carolyn and I sneaked out to the car after half an hour to have another taste we'd mixed up ready in the needles before we left home. Boy Scout, always prepared.

The ceremony and the cremation were a blur: the only thing that stood out was the door sliding open and Dad's coffin rolling into darkness behind.

We arranged to come back for the ashes the next day, and drove home.

We scattered the ashes two days later, in the Murray River. We took them to his favourite fishing spot, and Mum watched as I climbed out on a fallen tree to empty the plastic box they had given us with the remains.

Carolyn and I spent another day in Rochester, helping Mum and making arrangements for the neighbours to help out once we were gone.

Finally, we had to leave when the heroin ran out. "We'll be back up in a week or two, Mum," I said. "Are you sure you'll be okay?"

"You go home," she said. "I'll be fine. Cousin Lee will be up on Thursday, and Sandra next door will keep an eye on me."

"Well, you call if you need anything," I said.

An hour later, we were on the road, on our way home. Stoned, as usual. I'd also conned some more money out of Mum. I had little in the way or ethics when it came to scoring, but I also had real trouble living with what I was doing every day to get by. The constant enigma. How to survive as a junkie and not do terrible things. I regret so much these days, but there is no way to change who I was then. All I can do is be the best I can now.

I missed Dad terribly, and I suppose I grieved at times, but the heroin swamped the feelings, burying them under a layer of blurred sensations. It was only years later that I would really face the loss and wish things could have been different. My main regret was that he could never see me get clean and pull my life together. My father was a good man. He worked hard every day of his life, and all I could do was waste it.

ON THE 'DONE (1997)

My habit got worse in a short period of time. We were using every day, and before long I started needing a taste every day rather than wanting one. Finally, after a few days where I tried to get some cash but couldn't, we decided enough was enough and went to see a doctor about getting on methadone. We were both really sick by that point.

It was Friday, and we hadn't slept since Sunday night. I'd gone to the local market and sold some stolen books on the weekend, but we hadn't been able to score since then.

All up, it was day four without heroin – day three and four are the worst. At nine in the morning I'd tried ringing my mum for some money, but she refused to send us any. I think she'd worked out I was lying to her. I can't blame her. Looking back, I'm glad she finally worked out how to say no.

I'd just walked back from the phone booth after calling. I collapsed on the bed next to Carolyn.

"Where can we get some fuckin' money from, darl?" I asked.

"There's nothing we can sell. I had a look while you were up at the phone. No luck with your mum?"

"Nah. She told me she hasn't got any," I said. I rolled over and curled up.

My legs were aching; I was covered in sweat and I felt totally fucked up. It's hard to describe to someone who hasn't experienced it before. I felt nauseous and had fever-chills. I felt like screaming. One minute hot, the next cold, but sweating all the time regardless. The ache was deep in the bones, like someone had set grubs loose inside my skeleton, and they were slowly boring through the centres of every bone and joint.

"We could see a doctor and get on the 'done," she said.
"How quick could we do it? D'ya think we'd get an appointment today?" I asked, looking at the clock. It was just after 9.30 in the morning. "I don't think I can stand another sleepless night feeling like this."

"Grab the phone book and ring the local chemists. They can tell us who the prescribing doctors are around here," she said.

Methadone is a synthetic opiate. It's taken on a daily basis by addicts to stop withdrawals. The process here in Australia seems to be much simpler than other countries. GPs can take a course in prescribing, and then work from either their private clinics or the public health clinics set up in most areas. Then, certain pharmacies give out the doses, for a weekly cost, which is much lower than running a habit. The opiates in 'done last longer than heroin or morphine, so only a daily dose in necessary.

According to the Alcohol & Drug Foundation here in Australia, using a legal drug like methadone helps 'to stabilise the lives of people who are dependent on heroin and other opioids, and to reduce the harms related to drug use'. Methadone dosages are closely monitored to take away the withdrawals and cravings of addiction without providing a 'high', and this allows people to get their lives back on track.

I walked slowly and painfully back up to the phone booth and rang a couple of chemists before I found one that ran a methadone service. They gave me a number for a doctor over on the Nepean Highway, just past Fletcher Road. I called and managed to get us an appointment for just before eleven. I went home and we got ready to go.

We arrived at the surgery early. The waiting room was half-full of other addicts. We knew a few people there, but no-one engaged with us so we talked until we were called in to see the doctor.

"I'm Dr Franks. What can I do for you both?" he asked.

Carolyn spoke up first. "We need to go on the methadone program."

"And you?" he asked, looking over at me.

"Yep. We're both addicts," I said.

"How much do you use a day?" he asked.

"About five or six deals a day," Carolyn said.

"Yeah," I said.

"Okay. I can get you on the program, but it might take a day or two," the doctor said.

"Why so long?" I asked.

"I have to send the request off to the Health Department, and get a permit back to allow me to prescribe it for you," Dr Franks said.

I felt shattered. I'd expected to get straight on it and leave from here to be dosed. Carolyn had explained that it would help the withdrawals pretty much straight away – an hour or two at the most.

"Let me make a call, and I can give you a time frame," the doctor said. He got up and left the office, motioning us to follow him and sit in the waiting room again.

"Fuck," I said to Carolyn once we'd sat down again. "How fucking long is this gonna take?"

"Last time I went on the program, it was done the same day," she said. "I thought this'd be the same."

We sat in the waiting room, shuffling feet and fidgeting legs to try and deal with the discomfort for about an hour and a half before we were called back in to see the doctor.

"I've spoken to the Health Department, and your permits have been approved. I'll write you both a prescription for twenty milligrams daily." He reached into a drawer and pulled out a prescription pad. "This should make you feel better, but you need to make another appointment to see me in three days so we can see how it's going." He filled out two prescriptions and handed them to us.

We walked about a kilometre down the road to the dispensing chemist to get our first dose.

The chemist had a sheltered counter for the methadone clients, to give a semblance of privacy. Carolyn went first, and then it was my turn. I had no idea what to expect. The pharmacist brought me a plastic cup with a small amount of amber fluid in the bottom. I drank it down. It had a strange, bitter taste. I refilled the cup from a jug of cordial on the bench to make sure I got the whole dose and to get the taste out of my mouth. We had to pay each week in advance, at five bucks a day or thirty bucks for the week. It was a lot cheaper than smack.

By the time we'd caught the bus home, I was starting to feel a little fuzzy. The withdrawals no longer affected me, and I actually felt a little stoned. It wasn't as strong a feeling as heroin, but it was vaguely similar. I was happy to have lost the pain and discomfort of withdrawal.

Every day – seven days a week – we went to the chemist to pick up our 'done and every day I felt stoned for the rest of the night. Carolyn had to increase her dose, but mine was keeping me stable. Once the first week was over, I stopped feeling stoned from it and just felt better. I was more than fine with that most of the time.

After six months, we were each prescribed two take-away doses a week. During this 'maintenance therapy' we continued to use, just not every day like before but, because of the methodone, we needed a bigger taste to get high.

Life went on, nothing much changed. We were still addicted. The 'done may have cost a tenth of the price of smack, but if we missed a dose or two, we got just as sick.

The chemists were like dealers – no money, no dose. The only difference was the legality.

DEALING (1997-98)

I remember the first time I saw Big Jim. Carolyn and I were in the lounge-room, smoking cones and watching Black Adder. We were on the two-seater couch and we both had a clear view of the street from the front window. I saw movement, so I glanced out and saw a massive guy walk past. He looked at least six-four and weighed maybe a hundred and forty kilos.

"For fucks' sake," I said, turning to Carolyn. "Someone's shaved a gorilla and taught it to walk upright."

She laughed. "Yep, looks about right," she said.

Not long after, he walked past when I was outside in the front yard picking up rubbish passers-by must have thrown in. We started talking. It turned out his name was Jim and he'd just moved in up the street.

Jim's wife had died of a blood clot on the brain. He'd been left to raise their two kids alone.

This was a major lifestyle re-adjustment for a guy who'd been heavily involved in underworld circles for many years; much of that time spent as an enforcer for some really heavy Serbian gangs.

Jim had served in Europe, in the Serbian armed forces, one of thousands of infantry soldiers given the dirtiest jobs. In the Serbian war, those jobs were pretty dirty.

He was a titled heavyweight kick-boxer as well. Jim was a monster that not many would dare to cross. I sure as hell knew he'd kill me if I ever had cause to fight him.

The death of his wife had changed him to a large degree. He suddenly found himself the only parent for his two kids, Ashleigh and Luke, and had to make some tough choices.

Jim and I became good friends, and Carolyn's kids got along well with his, so we tended to play-group them to keep them occupied. Jim was an addict, so we often scored together when we could. We had a car at this point and Jim didn't, so we sometimes drove him into Frankston to get his 'done.

One day I got a letter from Social Security telling me that they'd been paying me less than they should have for a long while, so there was a deposit of nearly seven hundred bucks put into my account.

"Carolyn. I've got an extra seven hundred in my account. D'ya wanna go score?" I asked.

"Fuck, yeah," she said. "Let's go before the kids get home from school."

The car wasn't running right at this point, so we called a taxi and went to Springvale, the nearest major heroin centre. On the way, we decided to buy big, a gram if we could. It took an hour to find someone who was willing to sell us that much at bulk price, and it still cost around four hundred bucks. We went into the toilets behind the shopping strip for a taste, and then caught a taxi home with most of the gram left.

"Should we make up a few deals with the rest?" Carolyn asked.

"Good idea," I said. "We could get most of our cash back and buy some more."

We made up six caps, and had another taste before I caught the bus into Frankston to see if anyone was looking to score.

I got off the bus and looked around to see who I knew. Marty was across the road, just leaning against a light pole. I walked over.

"Hey, Marty. Wanna score?"

"No-one's around," he said. "I've been here half-an-hour already."

"I've got some caps," I told him.

"Fuck, yeah," he said.

My first sale. The only way is up from here.

I sold the rest of the gear in about an hour. There were always people around looking to buy. Everyone knew me. It was too easy.

The next day, I did it all over again. We still had nearly four hundred bucks left, so I called a guy I knew who sold larger amounts of gear at even better prices than our first buys in Springvale. I met him near the local shops. My life as a heroin dealer had begun.

It was a Friday morning. I stood at the bus stop, fidgety and worried. If the cops were gonna grab me, now was the time. I had a quarter-gram of heroin in my coin-pocket. I'd just scored it for a hundred and forty bucks from James, an Asian guy I knew who did good sizes for reasonable prices. Everyone else I knew charged at least one-fifty.

The bus pulled up and I got on, finding a seat down the back. Soon enough, I'd reached the Mahogany Avenue shops, right near our house. I got off the bus and almost ran the last fifty metres, anxious to have a taste. The sweat was pouring off me when I got inside to find Carolyn already had the equipment ready on the coffee table.

"About fuckin' time," she said.

"I was as quick as I could," I said. "You know what James is like. He was late again."

Two fresh, unopened syringes were laid out on the coffee table, next to a spoon and a glass of water. There was a razor-blade and three pieces of foil ready to wrap the deals I needed to sell.

I sat down next to her, gave her a kiss on the lips and dragged the foil-wrapped package from the depths of my pocket.

Opening it up to reveal the white rock inside, I used the blade to cut it in half, putting one half aside for the deals we'd sell to get the one-forty needed to score, and putting the other half in the spoon.

I mulled up and handed Carolyn her syringe.

After we had our tastes, I cut the remaining smack into three deals and wrapped them in foil. I grabbed a bag of water balloons, sealing each foil-wrapped deal inside one for safety. Now I could keep them in my mouth, ready to swallow if the cops tried to grab me.

"I'll be back once I sell these," I said.

"Be careful," she warned as I hugged her and left. Soon enough, I'd sell the deals for forty or fifty bucks each and buy some more.

When I got back to Frankston, I got off well before the train station, opposite the Frankston Loan Company, to try and avoid the attention of the cops.

In half-an-hour, I'd sold the three caps and rang James again.

By putting some money aside each time we sold out, and then adding some from Carolyn's pension, over the next few days we ended up with enough cash to buy a gram at a time, and our habit rose accordingly. I'd stand in front the train station, in the outdoor mall or just walk around the block a few times, depending on customer activity and the cops.

Day after day, the same routine: score, hit, make up deals to resell, and then back to Frankston to sell the new lot so I could start all over again.

I did this at least five times a day – every day.

The Frankston cops were well aware of what was going on with all the drugs on the streets, but there were so many of us and so few of them. We all knew who they were. Plainclothes were useless unless they brought in new faces from other suburbs.

Unlike a lot of smack areas, the dealers in Frankston

were predominantly Caucasians. We still stood out like sore thumbs to those in the know, although some of us were more concerned with appearance than others.

Addicts are notoriously unkempt. After lying awake in agony all night, the last thing you feel like doing is taking the time to shower and dress well. Most didn't bother, but I believed it made sense to try and blend in as much as possible.

There's always that old devil pride, too. Most junkies lose that early on in the game, but I have always been aware of how others see me. I could never bear to go out smelly and dirty unless I was so sick I just didn't see another choice. There have been times I've been ashamed of how I looked, but those times I was so sick that I didn't care until after having a taste and then had to travel home feeling okay but looking like shit.

I scored my grams through a variety of sources. Sometimes locally in The Pines, sometimes in surrounding beachside suburbs and sometimes in the closest heroin Mecca, Springvale.

Springvale was comprised of Asian communities, encompassing a plethora of cultures and ethnicities – Vietnamese, Laotian, Indonesian and a multitude of others.

Amongst the refugees there were people with criminal pasts, and they brought their traits and connections with them to Australia. You also have second-generation kids of refugees, unable to fit into school and feeling isolated due to racism and the whole 'White Australia Policy' thing.

Asian gangs quickly gained a stronghold in these communities, the parents too scared of authority to go to the police, and the kids too socially-unacceptable to fit in anywhere else. The gangs have an easy time targeting children of refugees as members, because the kids are already traumatised and marginalised by their life experiences. They make good use of the people who have no other options, or at least feel that way.

Dealers walk along the main shopping strips, ready for all the customers that spring up almost with the sun. It was easier for the Asian dealers to blend in here, and everyone else were just junkies looking to score.

It was harder for the police to operate covertly in these areas. Even in Caucasian smack suburbs they stood out, so they were even more apparent in Asian suburbs. Nearly all junkies can pick a cop trying to look like they're not a cop.

There are a million subtle mannerisms, ways of looking at things, ways of sitting and standing. Ways of simply 'being' that make it hard to disguise as a druggie.

Life went on, dealing and using, until Rochester Hospital rang me early one morning. Mum had had a turn and was admitted for observation. She was fine, but it was handy. By telling Social Security that Mum was in hospital and I needed to go see her, I'd convinced them to give me a chunk of money. I felt guilty lying to Social Security to get some cash, but it was a way to get some quick drugs, and addicts are masters at justifying their actions. I quickly pushed the guilt aside and concentrated on scoring. I've always been great at compartmentalising my emotions and guilt. I guess that was a result of my abuse and having to push those feelings aside.

I decided to buy two grams. Street dealers don't carry that much or sell that in one amount, so I needed to get hold of a bigger player. I parked at Springvale Library and walked down the street. I passed two or three dealers within a few yards of the Coles supermarkets, but no-one wanted to help me score such a big amount. Eventually, I found a guy who said he could organise it, and followed him a couple of blocks away from Springvale Road.

"What's your name?" he asked.

"Geoff," I answered. "What's yours?"

"John," he said. "I seen you 'round here before, yeah?"

"Yeah, mate. I come here all the time to get on," I told him.

"You not a cop, are ya?"

I pulled up my sleeve and showed him the needle-marks on my arm. "Nah, mate. I'm no cop."

"You look like cop, that's all," he laughed. It wasn't the first time I'd heard this, and it likely wouldn't be the last.

He made a call on his mobile phone, and arranged for his dealer to meet us in ten minutes.

Twenty minutes later, the dealer turned up in a little Toyota Supra. John made me wait while he went over to talk to the guy, then beckoned me over.

There were three guys in the car, two Asians in the front and a white guy in the back. They all looked stoned.

"You want two gram?" the front passenger asked.

"Yeah, mate," I said. "Two grams."

He reached under the seat, pulled out a black leather zip-up bag, and opened it. He rummaged inside and pulled out a plastic baggie with two foil packages inside.

"You got cash? Six hundred?" he asked.

"Yep," I said. I pulled the money out of my pocket and handed it over. He handed me the baggie after he counted the cash to make sure it was all there.

I stuffed the baggie down the front of my t-shirt.

"Can I grab a phone number for you guys?" I asked. "I'm gonna want more, and often."

"Yeah, man," the passenger said. He pulled a slip of paper from the same leather bag and handed it to me. "You call us, yeah?"

"Yeah, mate. I will. What hours?" I asked.

"All hours. Nothing smaller than a gram," he said. "The name's Paul."

I stuffed the number in my pocket. "Thanks, Paul."

The window rolled up as they drove away.

I turned to John. "Where can we go for a taste?" I asked. It's standard to chop-out someone who helps you score.

"I got a place a few blocks away," he said. We walked to his place and went inside. I could smell Asian food and cat-shit. It was a real mess.

He got some water and a spoon.

"Got any freshies?" I asked. I had one clean fit.

"Yah, man. I'll get 'em," he said. He walked out of the room and came back in a minute or so with a box of syringes.

I mulled up a big rock and gave him a good taste, although I had more.

"Thanks, mate," he said as I packed the rest of the gear away while the numbness came on. I walked back to the car and drove home. Carolyn had a taste when I got home, and I had a bit more, even though I didn't really need it. We made up the resale rocks and I went off to Frankston to do the business. By the afternoon, we'd sold the gram and used the rest of ours, so I drove back to score another two grams from Paul.

STRIPSEARCHED (1998)

I knew most of the dealers in Frankston personally, and knew the faces of the rest. The majority were street dealers like me, but some dealt from home.

These guys usually sold larger amounts than those on the street. Often street-level dealers sold one-shot amounts. One rock, usually well under point one of a gram, for forty or fifty bucks. I made mine a little bigger than most to try and attract customers. The whole idea was to get rid of the smack as quickly as possible to reduce the risk of getting busted.

I kept the deals wrapped in water balloons. I once ran out of these, so I foiled all the deals, wrapped them in squares of plastic from a shopping bag and sealed them with a cigarette lighter. I couldn't risk putting them my mouth this time, in case the seals were not perfect and spit seeped in and contaminated the deals and cost us money or customers.

I placed them in the lining of my jacket, through a small hole I'd cut inside one of the pockets. I went to the trouble of pushing them all the way to the back, hoping that would be enough to make a difference if I was hassled.

I caught the bus into town, and as I got off, two cops grabbed me. There was nothing I could do as they dragged me back into the bus shelter. They held me in place by the arms and pushed me down onto the seat. An unmarked cop car pulled up, and another, older, cop got out.

"Right, cunt," the old one said. "We have reason to believe you're carrying illegal substances. Get the jacket off. The hat, too."

I did as they said. The one on my left grabbed my baseball hat while the older cop took the jacket. The third one continued to hold onto me.

Old-Cop looked at me. "Anything sharp or dangerous in here, boy? Anything that's gonna stick me?"

I shook my head in the negative.

He looked at me even harder. "If I *do* get stuck, you're fucked."

I nodded in reply. "Nothing in there that'll hurt you, officer," I said.

The other cop searched the hat's lining, while Old-Cop checked the pockets of my jacket. I tried not to look at him, hoping he wouldn't find the gear. Hat-Cop told me to take off my shoes and socks. I obeyed. I noticed Old-Cop feeling along the lining below the pockets. I quickly looked away, knowing I was fucked.

After checking my footwear, Hat-Cop told me to take off my hoodie. Again, I did as I was told.

He threw it onto the seat in the shelter. "Take off your shirt."

I did.

He barely glanced at it as he threw it near the hoodie. "Now get your jeans off," he said.

"What?" I looked at him in shock. Cops weren't allowed to strip people in public.

"Get your fucking jeans off now!" he said.

"Am I under arrest? 'Coz I don't think– "

"I don't give a fuck *what* you think, cunt," he roared. "Get your fucking jeans off now or you *will* be under arrest."

I did what he asked. If they took me to the station, they'd find the gear for sure.

I stood shivering and blue while the coppers searched through all my clothes once more. I started to sweat a bit when one of them again checked the jacket pockets and even started feeling the bottom lining, but he never went all the way to the back.

By now, a small crowd had gathered to watch.

The cops handed me back my clothes and let me get dressed, clearly upset they'd failed to find what they knew I was holding.

I figured they must have watched me score and go home to make it up, and then decided to bust me with the capped-up gear to get me for dealing.

Not this time, guys.

Just a very embarrassing impromptu strip in the main street of Frankston.

I went and sold the caps they'd failed to find, and Carolyn and I had a good laugh about it when I got home. I made sure I bought some more balloons on the way.

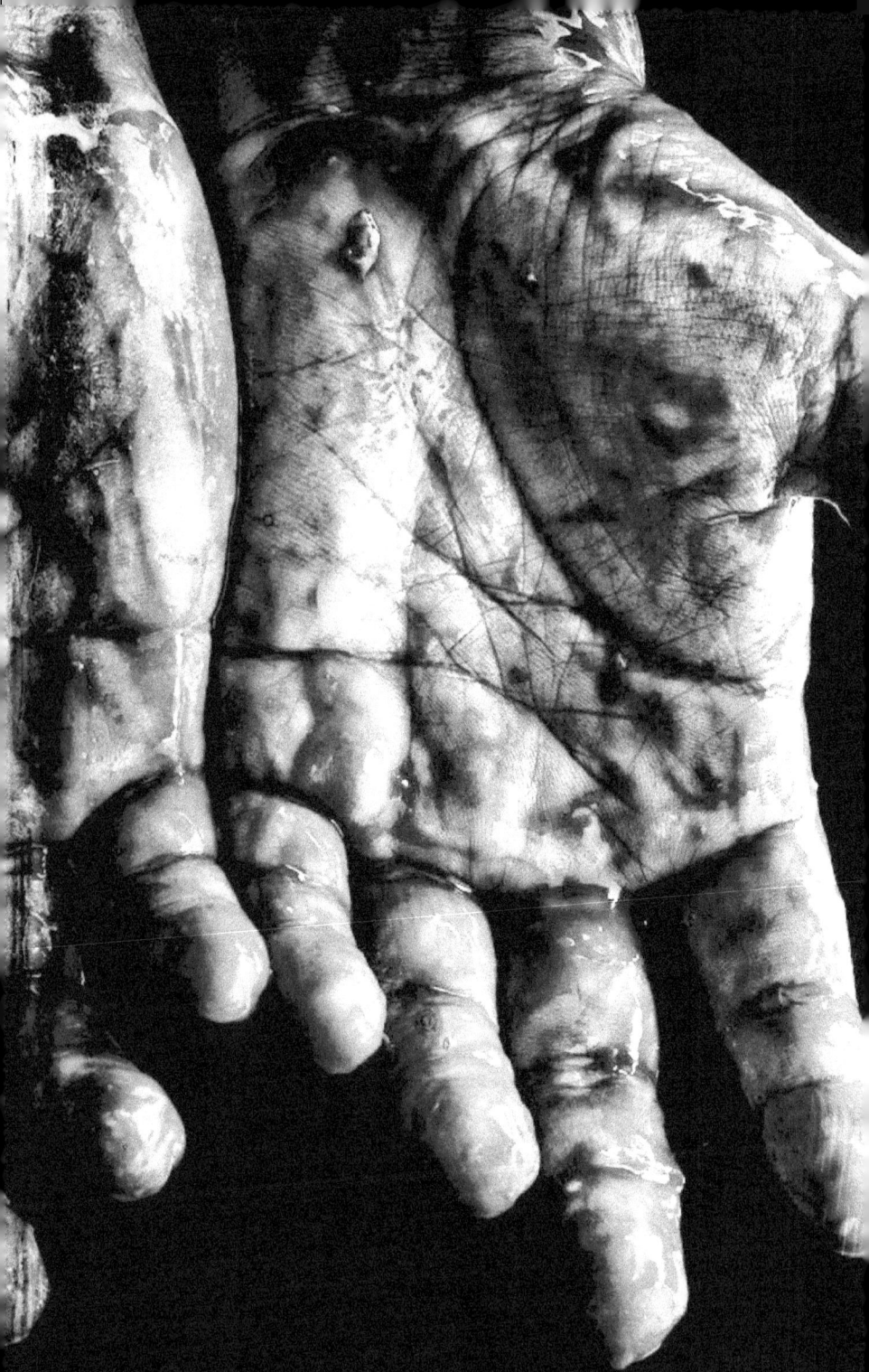

MACHETES AND KNIVES (1998)

Arriving in Springvale one afternoon, I witnessed a horrifying event. Some desperate junkie must have tried to rip off a dealer behind the train station. I got off the train and as I walked down the ramp past the deserted ticket-office I saw a crowd gathered down the far end of the car-park.

A group of Asians had surrounded someone, hacking at him with sticks and knives. He was curled up on the ground, covered in blood.

I thought I recognised one of the attackers, and it was someone I wanted to score from. As I approached, the victim leapt to his feet and limped down the street away from the station. He didn't look back, and the crowd let him go, calling out abuse and laughing, patting each other on the backs. I could hear sirens in the distance, so the police were on their way. The Asian guys scattered and ran, anxious to avoid the cops

I never found out what it was all about, but I remember looking down at the pools of blood to see the tip of a finger, curled-up like a bug in the red. I staggered off and found another dealer in the underpass.

The smack scene is steeped in violence, and this was a lesson to never piss off these dealers. I never did rip-offs, and things like this pushed home that it was a good thing to remember.

Some guys think they're tough enough to be stand-over men, usually sick junkies who get desperate enough to prey on other addicts. It works for a while, but there's always someone tougher or stronger.

I remember a guy rang me up and asked me to come over to his house. I'd never trusted this guy so I only ever took one or two deals over there with me whenever I went, and usually got him to meet me in town somewhere neutral if I could. He was a big bloke, much bigger than me and he'd done a lot of time in gaol. He was trouble.

When I arrived, he had no money and asked me for credit. He still owed me forty bucks from a previous score, so I said no and got up to leave. By the time I reached the entry hall he had grabbed a steak knife from the kitchen and stepped in front of the door.

"Gimme the fuckin' dope or I'll fucking shiv ya, ya cunt." He took a step toward me and I took a step back into the living room.

"You're gonna stab me over fifty bucks, ya fucking rat?" I said.

"Too fuckin' right, cunt, now gimme the gear... now!"

I reached into the coin pocket of my jeans and pulled out the only cap I'd brought in with me this time, throwing it at him.

"I hope you fucking OD on it, ya cunt. Don't ever fucking call me again!"

I walked out to the car and got in, considering picking up Jim to come over and sort him out.

Fuck it. I'll just never serve the cunt again.

It's worth fifty bucks to get rid of customers like that.

I saw him on the street a week later and he crossed the road to avoid me, looking down at his feet as he went.

MOVING UP (1999)

I began selling a lot on the street and through my mobile phone. It was business as usual; all the regular street dealers were around, but something else had changed, something that would affect me in ways I couldn't even imagine at the time. A new crew of smackheads had arrived in town.

There were two couples, Islanders that had just moved down from Sydney. The two guys – Peter and Mark – started selling on the street near me, so I got to know them pretty quick. The gear they sold was always good and the sizes were better than anyone else, nearly double those of some of the scungier dealers.

Soon enough, I was selling all of my deals to regular customers and then buying some off the new guys if I needed. For each two I bought from them, we could resell some and still have a small taste ourselves. Soon enough, they pulled me aside for a chat. They wanted to move away from street level dealing and asked if I wanted to buy larger quantities from them. The only reason they had started dealing on the streets, they said, was to get to know the people in the local scene.

We ended up going for a drive and parking behind the shopping area near the beach. They offered to give me an eighth of an ounce on credit, but had difficulty splitting the quarter ounce they had. I ended up taking home the whole thing, on the understanding I'd call them tomorrow and pay fifteen hundred bucks. Carolyn couldn't believe her eyes when I pulled out seven grams of heroin and laid it on the table.

"What the fuck?" she exclaimed.

"Those Islanders want us to buy from them from now on. A quarter-ounce at a time," I told her.

"Fuck," she said. "Let's have a taste."

I mulled up a nice big rock, and we got as stoned as hell. The gear was good.

We had more smack than we'd ever seen in one place before. We made up a heap of deals, and I went down the street, still reeling from the giant taste we'd had. I even vomited on the bus.

I sold ten deals in an hour, and went back home again with nearly four hundred bucks in my pocket.

When I got home, Carolyn and I decided to upgrade the operation by selling to the street level dealers by phone and car rather than continue selling on the street.

We decided to sell three-point deals – each deal three tenths of a gram – for a hundred bucks or half-grams for one-fifty, a much better price than anyone else in the area. To get those kinds of prices you either had to go to Richmond, the source of heroin for most of Melbourne, or you had to know good people in Springvale.

I had a new pre-paid mobile – set up under a false name – which I kept open from seven in the morning until midnight, seven days a week. Unlike other dealers, I never kept anyone waiting too long, and I did my best to make sure I always had gear.

This was better service than most addicts were used to. Soon enough I had more clients than I could poke a stick at.

The phone started ringing as soon as I switched it on and kept it up until at least half past midnight. I usually kept it switched on until I went to bed, and I always tried to refuse anyone who called outside office hours, but I remembered what it was like to hang out all night. I didn't really have the heart to say no sometimes, especially if I liked the caller.

I thought about the fact that I now had a lot less control over who used my gear. When I was selling on the street, I made sure only regular users bought from me. I wouldn't sell to kids or first-timers, as I didn't want anything like that on my conscience. Now, I had no idea who was shooting up the gear I was selling. I justified this by telling myself that the responsibility was on the street-dealers. Once the gear was out of my hands, I held no guilt regarding what happened to it. Not really true, though. Not at all. I see that now.

❧ ❧ ❧

I was getting the stuff on tick – on credit – and that's never a good thing. Addicts are always after credit themselves – most people will always be a few dollars short or wanting to trade stolen goods for gear instead of cash. Some would try to steal from dealers, but I had a remedy for that. I had Jim.

He worked as my minder in exchange for free drugs. Word got around that if you crossed me, you crossed Jim. No-one wanted to be on the receiving end of Jim's anger, so it kept me safe from rip-offs most of the time. Dealers face lots of stand-over men, guys who'd rather intimidate than pay for their drugs. I was a big guy, and could certainly stand up for myself if I had tried, but Jim was a monster everyone was afraid of. For a while there, he was my monster.

Trade was different. Sometimes I would take trade goods, as it always worked out in my favour. A month or two prior, Carolyn had started training to be a naturopath in Melbourne. It was always a struggle to meet the tuition costs, but we managed. It helped that we didn't have to find hundreds of dollars a day for our drugs. The dealing was paying for our own use and showing a profit as well.

She was away each day, studying in the city while I sold drugs to support us.

Seven days a week, eighteen hours a day I sold heroin to the dealers and more cashed-up drug users of Frankston.

I was seeing the Islanders at least five or six times a

day, picking up an eighth or a quarter-ounce each time. Two grand's worth of heroin every day. Because I had been given the first quarter on tick, I was always behind, paying for the last lot while picking up the next.

One time they were going away for a week, so they left me three ounces to last us while they were gone. It didn't, though, which is always the way with addicts. Enough is never enough.

I was lucky that something else fell into our hands at just the right time.

MORPHINE (1999)

A woman we knew reasonably well, a smoker that we gave cheap buds to now and then, gave us a large amount of morphine and pethidine. Her husband had suffered from terminal cancer, and when he died she was left with nearly fifty thousand milligrams of the drugs in liquid form.

She didn't want it in the house, and knew we were users, so she just decided to give it to us. All of a sudden, at no cost, we had around five hundred vials of hospital-grade opiates. Each vial was equal to about a hundred dollars' worth of heroin. Each vial was worth around seventy bucks on the street.

Suddenly we were in junkie heaven.

We used it ourselves and we sold it to people who didn't mind the pins and needles and hives that came with shooting up morphine or pethidine. It was a thing unique to that particular kind of opiate, and was unavoidable. Patches of skin over your entire body would start to prickle about ten seconds after pushing the plunger in and sending the stuff through the bloodstream and into the brain. Even though I know heroin becomes morphine in the bloodstream, injecting straight pharmaceutical opiates always felt much worse than heroin did.

Personally I didn't enjoy the morphine rush anywhere near as much as smack, but the end result was still the same. Feeling stoned and not hanging out.

These vials lasted about three weeks before everything was gone and it was back to business as usual with normal heroin. This gave us a chance to get ahead on the bills and utilities, as well as fill the cupboards and the fridge to the very brim. It was a bad time masquerading as good.

After it was gone, it was back to the same old shit, but in a much better financial position.

NEARLY CAUGHT:
THE BEGINNING OF THE END

I was driving a few friends to score. I couldn't get hold of the Islanders, so I rang another dealer named Joel. We all had our own money and were buying bulk-lots of at least a quarter gram. We were due to meet him in Oliver's Hill, a more affluent area part of Frankston. We parked in a residential street, trying to look inconspicuous.

Eventually Joel turned up in his red Rav 4 wagon. The deal was done, and we sat there as the others started mulling up in the car and I made up a whack for Carolyn and myself. After I had my taste, movement behind the car caught my eye and I glanced in the rear-view mirror as I sucked up Carolyn's taste into a fresh fit. I just about shit myself when I saw a divvy-van pulling to a stop right behind us.

"Fuck! *Cops!*" I yelled, frantically recapping the fit I was holding and slipping it into the pocket space on the driver's side door. I wrapped up the large heroin rock that was still on the centre console while I started the car with the other hand.

The divvy van's doors flew open as I took off up the street, only to find another car, unmarked this time, turned in to block our exit.

That's it. We're fucked.

I threw the foil-wrapped rock of smack into my mouth, although I had no balloon to wrap it in to protect it. Lucky I had only picked up a gram from Joel.

The divvy-van pulled up behind us, effectively blocking us in. I swallowed the gear just as two uniformed cops from the unmarked car motioned us out. We were searched and a few syringes were found on the others. Soon after that, they found the loaded fit I had put in the door pocket. One of the cops squeezed it out onto the ground, and the small amount of rock found on one of the guys was crushed underfoot.

I should have realised it was unusual behaviour; normally we would all be arrested for possession and taken back to the cop-shop. Instead, the gear they found was dumped and we were released.

I tried to throw up the rock I'd swallowed, and I managed it after a couple of tries. It was badly eroded from the moisture in my gut – mostly gone and totally useless – so I just swallowed it again. No point wasting it.

As I'd lost all the smack I had, and I needed to get more to take home to Carolyn. She'd be hanging out fairly soon if I didn't return with some gear.

I had no more money on me, so I rang Joel and arranged to meet with him again in fifteen minutes, halfway back to Frankston. I ended up getting another half-gram on tick and set off home as fast as I could.

I dropped the others off in Frankston and drove straight home. By then, I was really stoned from the large amount I'd swallowed. I knew it wasn't enough to kill me but it was such a waste.

I told her what had happened while she mulled up, and she thought it was strange they let us go. We both knew how the cops worked, from years of using drugs and hearing tales from other dealers. The only reason to let me go would be if another investigation was underway, and they didn't want to get in the way with small possession charges.

SURVEILLANCE (1999)

T he cop car was sitting halfway up the block, trying its best to look inconspicuous. It had been there on and off for days, and I did my best to act as though I didn't know they were watching me.

I did know, though. It was hard not to notice them. The fact that they were parked in the same spot every day made them stand out like buffalo balls on a budgie.

Stupid fuckin' cops.

I couldn't slow down on the business side of things, though. At this point I needed to sell at least three grand's worth of smack a day to cover our own ongoing habits. We were using about a third of everything we bought between us on a daily basis, and there was no other way to finance such a big habit. There didn't seem to be a way to change this situation, and it seemed as though our tolerance was only getting higher. On top of this, we were still on low-dose methadone.

The phone rang again. Another customer, there was never a shortage of buyers when it came to smack. I had to be careful with those police cunts watching me.

They would be looking to catch me selling. I knew it, and so did Carolyn. We couldn't see any way out, though, so it was just a case of hope for the best, expect the worst, and try to get by in the meantime.

I had cut off all the customers who I thought might betray me by buying from me with marked money or making a statement to the cops. I was taking all the precautions I could think of, but I knew it was just a matter of time. They had all the time in the world, as well as all the resources. All I had was a raging habit and the fact that I knew they were there.

"Those fucking cops are still sitting out there, darl."
Carolyn let the curtain drop back in place.

"I know. They must think we're stupid," I said. "I'll
take the back door. It shouldn't take long. John'll be there
waiting."

I snuck out over the rear fence and went to meet my
customer at the car park behind the shops around the
corner. I kept the gear in my mouth, five foil bundles safely
sealed in a water balloon. If the cops made a play for me,
I'd swallow them. The last deal left from the eighth ounce
of smack was safely concealed at home, also in a balloon so
Carolyn could swallow it if needed while I was out.

As I reached the alley that led behind the row of shops,
I looked out for John's white Honda. This guy had been
a good buyer, getting five hundred dollars' worth of gear
every day, and he always had the cash. Cash is king in the
world of drugs. I didn't know how he raised the money,
but I did know he worked long hours at whatever trade he
did.

Carefully checking behind me, I walked up to the
Honda and got in the passenger side. John was in his
thirties. Bright blue eyes and short black hair. His beard
made it harder to judge his age.

"Wassup, Joe?" John grinned, obviously glad the drugs
had arrived.

"Be careful, mate. The fuckin' jacks are following me,"
I mumbled as I spat out the bundles and handed them over
as he gave me a wad of cash.

"What?" He panicked, checking his mirrors and nearly
pushing me out the door.

"Relax. I left them watching the house and went out the
back." He seemed to calm a bit at that, but still got me out
of the car as fast as he could. I can't really blame him, and
I didn't want him busted. Good cash customers are hard to
find. Harder to keep.

I had a couple of customers who brought goods to trade, either from burglaries or shoplifting. One girl used to bring beautiful bed-sets, easily worth two or three hundred each, and trade them for a hundred bucks worth of smack. Another guy brought me an eight hundred dollar Citizen watch one time, along with a heap of other stuff including a PlayStation and about thirty games. For all of this, he only asked for a hundred bucks' worth of smack. We kept the stuff if we wanted it — like the PlayStation and the watch — and sold or gave the rest to people we knew. It was too dangerous to take it to pawn shops, as we had no idea where it had been stolen from.

The alley for deliveries behind North Richmond's Victoria Street shopping precinct. Hundreds of drug deals go down here every day of the year, mostly for heroin, but ice is catching up as it becomes more popular.

OVERDOSE AGAIN (1999)

Smack was always risky, both illegal and physically dangerous. I'd seen plenty of ODs, starting with Coz way back in McHenry St, but I soon had a chance to see it close up when we had a customer overdose in front of us.

Stan was a builder and a long-term addict. He came over to the house — he was one of the few customers I allowed access to my home — and bought two hundred bucks' worth. He asked to shoot up before he left, as he had to go straight back to work after lunch and didn't like to shoot up in the car. Too dangerous, he said. The cops might drive past.

Both the kids were at school, so we let him use the kitchen, and decided to have a taste ourselves. He threw a rock into the spoon.

"Careful with this gear, mate," I said. "It's a bit stronger than normal." This was true. The heroin had started getting stronger and stronger all the time. Good, but dangerous, as people tend to think they know their tolerance, yet don't take increased strength of the drugs into account.

"She'll be right, mate," he said, smiling.

I mulled up mine and Carolyn's, while Stan mulled up his own. We all had a taste, and immediately I noticed Stan's face go slack and his eyes close.

"Mate, are you okay?" I asked. No response. He slumped in his chair, his head drooping, drool falling from his mouth onto the table. I got up and went over to him. He was unconscious.

"John, wake the fuck up," I yelled, slapping him a couple of times. Nothing.

I pulled him from the chair to the floor. He was still breathing, but it was shallow. His face was pale, and his eyes rolled back into his head.

Carolyn grabbed his keys from the table. "I'll start the car. You bring him out," she said. I checked him again, and his breathing had become more laboured. He was only a small guy, so I picked him up and dragged him to the bathroom. I threw him in the shower, fully clothed, and switched on the cold water. After a second, he spluttered and his eyes opened slightly.

"John. Are you okay?" I asked.

"Wha...?" he mumbled.

"Mate, you had too much." I said. I turned off the water. He was soaked to the skin, but his colour was coming back a little.

"I'm fine," he said. "What the fuck are you doing? I'm fucking soaked!"

"You nearly stopped breathing," I said. "Look, if you feel okay, you need to get going." I helped him stand. "Naomi gets out of school early today, and you need to go."

He staggered out to the car, where Carolyn was waiting, car running in the driveway. She must have thought we'd need to drive him to the hospital. He got in his car, still soaked to the skin, and left. Ten minutes later, he pulled up out front. He'd left the rest of his smack on the table. I made it a rule to never let anyone except friends shoot up in the house ever again.

💉 💉 💉

We were covering our habits – for now – and sometimes even turning a slight cash profit without having to touch either of our Social Security payments to support our drug use. The fridge and cupboards were full. The kids had plenty of clothes for a change and there was cash in our pockets when we needed it.

We were doing okay, except for the surveillance.

In the days and weeks to come, I would see more and more signs that I was under observation: late model cars parked in unusual places in the street, other cars that seemed to be following me... it all seemed to fit.

I tried to be more cautious leaving the house: climbing over the back fence and cutting through the kindergarten behind us became my usual mode of exit and entry when meeting customers, but that limited me to walking and doing everything locally, a definite downside. The area we lived in was red-hot with coppers. Frankston North, The Pines, had been a military housing complex before being sold to the Housing Commission for low-income housing. When you lump a heap of low-income earners together in one area, you create an instant slum.

Sooner or later the cops worked out what I was doing and started posting a car in the back street, making sure they knew when I was going out. I went back to driving and watched my arse. I hoped that I'd find a way out of the corner I'd boxed myself into, but I couldn't see much chance of that. Smack is always a one-way street – there's little to no chance of going back, especially in one piece.

Front gate of The Bridge Detoxification Unit, situated behind high fences in Victoria Crescent Abbotsford. This Salvation Army place saved my life.

PART THREE

GETTING OUT 1999-2011

💉 💉 💉

"Desperation is the raw material of drastic change. Only those who can leave behind everything they have ever believed in can hope to escape."
~ William S. Burroughs

BUSTED (1999)

December, 1999, and the sun was bright in the morning sky as I pulled the Toyota over at Kananook train station. I was pleasantly stoned and on my first run of the day. I had picked up an eighth of an ounce of smack from my supplier earlier that morning, had a great big whack and then divided what was left into hundred dollar deals.

Carolyn had left for college and it was a beautiful day.

Gerry slipped into the passenger seat, as glad to see me as all addicts are glad to see their dealer. It was about seven-thirty in the morning, and he was my first customer of the day. As he went to close the door, I heard a screech of tyres from behind and looked in the mirror. There was a dark-blue Holden Commodore tearing around the corner, with at least two people inside. Straight away, I knew it was the cops. I freaked out.

I yelled at Gerry to hold on and slammed my foot down on the accelerator, taking off with a squeal as the cops headed toward me. Gerry hadn't even shut the door properly, but I had no time to worry about that, taking off up the street as the commodore closed in.

I grabbed the pill bottle I kept the gear in and poured the deals out into my lap, steering with the other hand as the Commodore crept up behind me and pulled out to overtake.

Throwing the multi-coloured bundles into my mouth and swallowing, I concentrated on keeping the Toyota on the road, trying to work out what to do next. I was scared as hell. The other car drew level with me and I looked over to see a cop pointing a gun at me and yelling, "Pull over. Pull the fuck over, or I'll fucking shoot you."

I barely paid any attention to him until I'd swallowed the entire amount I had with me, and then slowed down to stop. The Commodore pulled across in front me as I came to a halt, so I had nowhere to go if I tried to take off again. Gerry still hadn't put on his seat belt, and once we'd stopped, he tried to run. Two cops came from out of nowhere and tackled him to the ground, wrestling him onto his front and handcuffing him.

By that stage I had been dragged from the car by two more cops, and thrown handcuffed onto the road behind the Toyota. A marked cop car pulled to a screeching halt over my upper body.

I was pulled out from under the car. A couple of kicks to the ribs settled me down completely, and then they dragged me to the rear and threw me into the backseat. They searched my car from top to bottom, throwing things all over the nature strip of the house we'd stopped in front of. There were residents everywhere; standing in their yards, sipping coffee and chatting while they watched my life fall to pieces.

After about fifteen minutes, one of the detectives came to talk to me.

"Okay, fuckwit. Where's the gear." He scowled at me over the top of his glasses, trying to appear intimidating.

"I dunno what you're talking about, officer," I said.

"I have to inform you that you are under arrest for possession, use and trafficking of heroin, and that we've got a search warrant for the premises at 49 Forest Drive, Frankston North. I intend to execute this warrant now. You will accompany us during this search, and then be taken to the station, where you will be processed and charged. Do you understand?" He slapped me, more like a woman than the big tough cop he thought he was. "You're fucked, mate," he said.

After a little more fruitless searching through the car, they gave up and packed everything back into the boot of the Toyota. One of the uniformed cops got in to drive it to the station where a more thorough search would take place.

Two detectives got in the front of the cop car for the drive back to my place.

When we arrived, they dragged me inside and threw me on the couch, still handcuffed. They started to search the place. They tore everything open and emptied stuff all over the floor.

They even tipped over the fridge to look behind it.

"C'mon guys, give us a break and take it easy, will ya?" I said. I didn't want Carolyn to come home from college to this god-awful mess. Then I remembered we'd arranged for her mother to pick up the kids from school and bring them home today.

Shit!

I had to let Carolyn know what was happening. The cops had emptied both the bedroom drawers, hundreds of new and used syringes scattered all over. There was the bong kicked over in the lounge. The whole house was filthy, and on top of the coffee table was our copy of the search warrant, with 'Search for drugs – Heroin –, proceeds of crime, drug paraphernalia' highlighted on the front.

I was sweating like crazy, worried they'd find something I'd stashed and forgotten about.

Despite the rather aggressive search, they found nothing at the house. It was all in my stomach, safely ballooned, or so I hoped.

After they finished tossing the house, they took me back to the station.

What now? Prison?

I knew I was in some deep shit.

The divvy van pulled around the back of the Frankston cop shop. We pulled up outside the rear door. Two cops opened the back of the van and dragged me out by the jacket. When we got inside the station, they threw me into a small interview room and took off the handcuffs.

"Hey, boys...what about my phone call?" It was as if I hadn't even spoken.

As they left the room, I massaged my wrists to try to get some circulation going. The door swung shut with a thud.

I was alone, and all I could think about was how sick I was starting to feel. I knew I had enough in my stomach to keep me comfortable, if I had a chance to get to it. I was sure the cops in the car had seen me swallowing it, but nothing had been said. I could almost feel it in there. If only I'd had time to unwrap one of the deals before swallowing it, I'd be feeling great by now.

I waited nearly two hours before anyone came to see me. Lucky I had gone to the dunny before I left to meet up with Gerry, else I might have had to take a piss in the corner of the interview room.

The sound of a key in the door made me look up. The door opened and the two detectives that had arrested me walked inside, wheeling in a tape deck on a trolley.

"G'day, Geoff. How's things?" the taller of the two said. He had a heavy build, with dark hair parted neatly on the right and blackheads all over his nose. His partner was a couple of inches shorter but just as stocky, with light red hair and a jowly, pig-like face. He looked irritated.

I looked at both of them from my side of the table, and didn't say a word.

"Where's the fuckin' gear, cunt?" Piggy didn't seem one for small talk.

"What you talkin' 'bout?" I grinned at Piggy, amused to see him grow even redder at my sarcastic tone. "And where the fuck is my phone call?"

Blackhead answered me. "You're not in America, Geoff. But we can be nice. You'll get a phone call soon enough. Just answer a few questions and we'll get straight to it."

"I ain't saying a fucking thing until I can call the missus and organise to get the mess at home cleaned up before the kids get there. And that's fucking it. I know my rights." I crossed my arms and shut my mouth.

Blackhead looked at Piggy and turned back to me. "Fine, Geoff. But after this you talk to us, okay?" They both got up and opened the door, gesturing me out into the corridor where a couple of phones hung on the wall. I called Carolyn's mobile.

"Hello?" Her voice sounded subdued, so she must have been in class.

"It's me. Fuckin' cops grabbed me. I'm in the jack-shop at Frankston. They searched the house, and it's a fucking mess. You need to get home and clean up before your mum gets there with the kids."

"What? Serious?" Carolyn sounded shocked, but it sank in soon enough and she told me she would leave class and go straight home. I asked her to bring me up a change of clothes, some ciggies and a toothbrush, then told her I loved her and hung up.

Blackhead and Piggy took me back to the interview room and sat me down, drawing up their own chairs on the other side of the table. Piggy reached over and switched on the tape decks.

Blackhead shuffled a manila folder full of paper open onto the desk. "We know you use heroin, Geoff, and we know you sell it. Make it easy on yourself and tell us all about it," he said.

"I want a lawyer. I know how you guys force people to confess to shit they never did." That was it. My version of the 'no comment' interview.

Piggy slammed his fists to the table, shaking it in the brackets that bolted it to the floor. "You fucking cunt. We gave you a phone call. Now you pull this shit?"

Blackhead was the more reasonable one. "We've been watching you for a while now, Geoff," he said as he stood up and walked around the table. "When you were dealing on the street down near the train station, we even got a plain-clothes officer to buy some heroin from you. We have the lab results here on what you sold us, and that by itself is enough to put you away." He leaned over a bit and stared at me.

Fuckin' hell.

"But then you moved up in the world, didn't ya? You started selling to the street dealers." He grabbed my chair and leaned in even further. "We have a statement from one of your regular customers that you supply him with heroin on a daily basis. How much have you been selling lately?" he asked. "About half an ounce a day, we reckon. Come on, we know what's really going on, so don't try to fuck with us." He walked back around the table and took his seat.

I just stared straight ahead, silent. I was breathless and sweating hard. I knew I was fucked, but I also knew I might get off a bit easier if I kept my mouth shut. I was scared to go to gaol, but at the same time I knew that's where I'd likely end up.

Piggy leaned forward, his breath like dog shit. "You can help us, and you along with it, or we can fuck you so hard you'll never walk right again."

I had to keep up a brave front, or these guys would walk all over me. I leaned even closer into him. "I didn't know you cared, Piggy. I hope you do 'reach around' at least?"

He leant over the table and grabbed me by the throat, but Blackhead pulled him back. "We've got this cunt any way you look at it, boss. Don't let him get to you," he said. "The other guy we grabbed with him has already talked." I shuddered a little at this, knowing that there was little loyalty between crims these days. Most would give you up in a second to get out of a charge.

Piggy looked at me with barely concealed hatred. "You're fucked, cunt. Fucked!" He got up and stormed out. Blackhead turned off the tape recorders. He turned to me. "You shouldn't rile him up, son. It's no good for his blood pressure."

Blackhead left, and I settled back into the chair, trying not to think about anything at all. It worked, and I think I dozed off.

The next thing I knew, the door opened again, and Piggy came in by himself. He turned and locked the door behind him. This didn't look good. He had a grin on his face that could only mean trouble.

"Guess who I just spoke to, cunt?" If possible, his grin grew even bigger. "I think the Department of Human Services is pretty interested in two kids being brought up in the house of a drug dealer. Bad influence and all that shit. Don't you think?"

I froze, and felt light-headed. Now I knew why he was grinning. I knew he had me. I couldn't let the DHS get involved. Carolyn had already lost her kids once, and was lucky to get them back. I knew she wouldn't survive losing them again.

"Get your mate, Piggy, and let's get this over with. I'll make a statement."

The words left a bad taste in my mouth. Where I grew up, you never co-operated with the cops. Never. But I couldn't have DHS involved, or it would get ugly. The department was a joke most of the time, but once they got their teeth into something, they never let go. I thought I may have a way out of this without anyone doing time because of me, but I'd have to do a good job conning these fuckers.

Piggy left and came straight back with Blackhead and the two tape decks in tow.

"This is an interview between Detective Sergeant Adam Hughes and Geoff Brown, conducted at Frankston police station on the twelfth of October, 1999. Also present is Detective Constable Emmanuel Barnes. We are conducting an investigation into the use and supply of illicit substances, particularly heroin, in the Frankston area, and we wish to interview you in relation to these matters. You are not obliged to do or say anything unless you wish to. Do you understand this?"

For another forty minutes the interview went on, with

me admitting to everything to keep DHS off our backs. We finally got the part they were most interested in.

"And where do you get the drugs that you then resell, Joe?"

"I buy them," I said. Piggy looked up from the sheet of paper he was reading and glared at me. "We know you buy it, but who do you buy 'em from?"

"An Asian guy in Carrum," I said. There was no way I was going to give Peter and Mark up to the cops. Blackhead leaned closer to me. "And his name is...?"

"He calls himself Michael, but I think his real name is Van or Tran or something..." If it looked like I was co-operating, they might believe me.

Piggy started to write in his notebook. "Can you describe him?" I looked over at him and said that he was short, thin and Asian, with black hair and brown eyes. Just a generic description, but it seemed to be enough. Piggy looked happier than I had seen him yet.

"And what sort of car does he drive?" he asked. I thought about it for a moment, trying to decide what was a popular brand of car with Asians, and came up with a blue Nissan, which also seemed to satisfy him. Things were going better than I thought. Maybe they would give me bail once they finished charging me. Fat chance.

I was formally charged with possessing heroin, trafficking heroin and possessing property being the proceeds of crime.

IN THE CELLS (1999)

When the interview was finished, they left me in that damn room for another four hours before they processed me, took fingerprints and a mugshot, and took me through to the cells. I was stressed out, and worried about Carolyn at home with no drugs. I'd always known I wouldn't get away with this forever, but now the reality set in. I was pushed through the door, and it slammed behind me.

Frankston cells were modern, as was the whole station. The lockup had a large common area, viewable from the corridor outside through a massive wall of Plexiglass. Off this space to the right were two cells, each with four stainless steel beds. Each bedroom had a sink and toilet alcove. There was also a shower area and bathroom separate. I knew the five blokes already in the common area. I'd sold gear to at least four of them. All the addicts in the area knew each other.

Before he left, the cop that had processed me asked if I wanted something to eat or drink. I jumped at the offer. By this stage, I was sweating and jumpy. When the food arrived, I took the tray into one of the bedrooms and lay down on an unoccupied bed.

Ignoring the microwaved toast, I grabbed the small packet of salt, and emptied it into the glass of water and gulped it straight down.

I went over to the toilet and stuck my finger down my throat. I started to gag, and I was worried it had been too long since I'd swallowed the gear, that it had already passed through my stomach, but my fear was unfounded.

As I chucked up, I saw the coloured bundles of smack hitting the water in the dunny. I scooped them up, counted (all ten three-point deals had come back up), rinsed them off, then stuffed them back into my mouth. Now I felt better: as long as I had some smack, I wasn't as anxious. It was a load off my mind to have the bundles out of my gut and in my mouth.

I moved back to the bed and covered myself with the blanket for some privacy. I spat one of the bundles out into my palm and tore it open with my teeth. A small foil-wrapped block fell into my hand. I peeled open the foil and revealed a white rock of heroin inside. I swallowed it whole to avoid the taste as much as possible. In half an hour, I was stoned. Each of the deals was just under a third of a gram, enough to hold me for half a day, so I had enough to last five days without getting sick.

I lay back on the bed, hands under my head, and waited for it to kick in. Soon enough, I fell asleep as the drugs hit me.

I didn't fully understand a way out at the time, but I'd had some vague idea for ages I was going nowhere fast, and had been for years. This event, the arrest and subsequent prosecution, was to be the one thing that drove home the fact that I needed to change in a big way, that I had to find a way. I'd known deep inside for years that things were getting worse, especially after I started using heroin. Once I started dealing, I knew it was only a matter of time before I got busted, but the reality was worse than I could ever have imagined. I'd known that if I stayed on my current road to self-destruction, soon enough I *would* be destroyed, either dead or locked up in prison and wishing I was dead. It seemed the time had come.

🩉 🩉 🩉

I was locked up for four days before a magistrate granted me bail.

I spent a lot of the time I was awake thinking about the past.

Where I was, where I was going, what I was actually doing with my life.

Half of the time I was stoned out of my mind and the rest of the time I was bored shitless, yet at the same time, my mind raced.

No books, no TV – nothing to pass the time, so most of the days and nights were spent reliving my terrible choices that had led me here, or trying to work out how I could change my life. I wasn't stupid. I was a pretty smart guy, really. I'd shown in the past that I could do anything I set my mind to. I just hadn't really seen the potential for a normal life.

I loved drugs too much. I loved that high, that feeling as I pushed the syringe under my skin, as I pushed the plunger and let the drugs take me away from my emotions. But now, I finally had to face where I was going and what I was going to do with my life. It wasn't easy.

I shared the smack I'd smuggled in with the guys in my cell and soon enough, the whole cell was on the nod with me. I was worried the cops would work out what was going on, but they didn't give a fuck what we did, as long as we behaved ourselves. They just fed us and unlocked the showers in the mornings.

My bail hearing was Monday morning at the Frankston Magistrate's Court. I didn't know if I'd make bail or get locked back up on remand until the court case. If I was remanded, I was in for one hell of a shit time from the certain withdrawal.

As I was led handcuffed into the courtroom from the lock-up, I looked in the public gallery for Carolyn. She was sitting near the front, head down but eyes locked on me. She looked sick. I'd had the smack I'd smuggled into the cells, but she'd had nothing for the whole weekend. I smiled at her, and nodded that everything would be okay. I tried to look confident, but I'm not sure how well I did. I was freaking out on the inside. I had no idea what would happen to me, but I was pretty sure I'd get gaol time for this. The cops had me over a barrel, and my confession would crucify me. I hadn't seen any choice, though. It was me, or Carolyn would lose her kids once more.

Because I'd made a statement, and because they thought I was being helpful, the police didn't oppose bail. They thought I'd given up a major supplier in the area. The magistrate allowed me bail on the condition that I reported to the police station at Frankston three times a week. It was a small price to pay for freedom. I let out a huge sigh of relief, the pent-up emotions finally letting go. I was free. At least until they locked me up for the dealing.

I was let out of the prisoner's dock and I moved to hold Carolyn.

"Relax, darl," I said. "Let's get the fuck out of here."

She'd parked in the courthouse car-park. We got into the Toyota and I told her we needed to get some fits.

"Fuck that," she said. "We need to go score first. I feel like shit!"

I smiled and poked out my tongue, two ballooned packages sitting there in plain view.

Her eyes bulged. "You fuckin' ripper," she said, smiling.

We drove across the road to the shopping centre underground car park, and had a taste as soon as we stopped the car.

TRYING TO GET CLEAN (1999-2000)

The threat of DHS involvement made us look at our lifestyle again. Although we'd always tried to do the best we could for the kids, they weren't blind and they weren't stupid; they knew something was going on, and had been for a long time.

Drugs were fairly common in the area we lived in, but some things still stood out to them. Little things add up, and the kids knew we had issues, but they had no idea how bad we were.

I knew my only chance to avoid a long gaol sentence was get as clean as I could.

When we got home from the bail hearing, Carolyn and I had a long talk about things.

"We can't deal any more, babe," I said to her. "If I get caught again before I go to court, I'm fucked."

"I know," she said.

"We need to get our shit together before court. I don't wanna go to gaol."

We had been on a low dose of methadone for the entire time, just picking up often enough from the chemist to avoid getting thrown off the program. If you don't get pick up for three days in a row, they assume you're using and cut you off. You need to go see a doctor to get back on. Now, we'd been using so much, we needed to go see our doctor and explain the whole thing. I expected the next few days to be hard.

One of the things I didn't expect, though, was trouble from my suppliers.

The weekend I was still in the cells, before I even got out on bail, they sent their sister around to our house to tell Carolyn that I needed to pay what I owed as soon as I got out. I hadn't given them up to the cops, and I thought that my loyalty would grant me a little time to pay. I was wrong. An hour after being released on bail, they'd called our home phone and told me I had twenty-four hours to fix them up.

I told them that I didn't have the cash.

"I'll pay soon," I said. "But if you keep up this bullshit, you can get fucked. I won't pay you at all."

"You better pay us, bro," Peter said.

"You'll get your money. Just stop acting like cunts." I hung up. I had to go meet my lawyer.

💉 💉 💉

There was no way I was getting out of all this without doing time. I was pleading guilty, but I wouldn't be leaving the court a free man – I was sure of it.

"Basically, Geoff, you're fucked," my lawyer told me at our meeting. "Don't expect to walk out of that courtroom without being handcuffed and on your way to lockup."

We went to the doctor's straight from the lawyer's office. We explained exactly what had happened, and the doctor contacted the Health Department and managed to increase our dose from twenty milligrams to eighty milligrams. If that didn't work, we could go see him in three days to get it put up even higher.

The increased dose barely kept me comfortable. For four or five days, I felt sweaty and irritable, suffered hot flushes and nausea. I had stomach and leg cramps and trouble sleeping. I didn't want to increase the dose any more than it was, so I put up with it. The temptation to use was extraordinarily powerful. I thought about scoring from the second I got up until the moment I went to bed. Usually throughout the whole night, too. I rarely slept for those days.

A week or so later, I started to feel better. It still took a second week for the sleep pattern to settle down, but the rest of the symptoms mostly went away.

☙ ☙ ☙

The next day the Islanders rang Carolyn's mobile (mine was kept as evidence by the cops) and threatened her. That was the last straw. We decided to get out of Frankston. Within two weeks, we'd organised absolutely fucking nothing, thanks to the hopeless bureaucracy of the Department of Housing. In the end, we had to fake domestic violence and a protection order to get them to move Carolyn from Frankston.

I tried to stay off the drugs, but it's nearly impossible to just stop.

We did cut down our usage a lot, but we still scored at least three or four times a week. I didn't seem capable of doing any better. The 'done helped with the physical stuff, but it didn't stop the voices in my head telling me I was worthless and weak. It didn't stop the feelings of shame I felt at who I was and the life I'd lived. It didn't stop the fear that lived inside me. All my life, I'd felt worthless. My life until then had only compounded those feelings. I still had a long way to go.

Top: Richmond graffiti art

Bottom: Syringes in a back alley. A common sight in any drug area.

MOVING (JANUARY 2000)

When the transfer finally came through, it was to Burwood, a much nicer area closer to the city. There were, like any partially-Housing Commission suburb, a few dysfunctional families in the area, but most of the residents were normal, working-class families.

We got a nice little townhouse. There was a massive university nearby, so there were a large number of students living in the area as well.

Pretty soon we met some people nearby that shared the same 'interests' as we did.

I wanted to get off the smack, but I still smoked dope all the time. I saw that as different: dope was a 'soft drug' compared to smack, and no worse than drinking. In a lot of ways, it seemed better to me. We continued to smoke as much as we could, and we still used smack a few times every week.

To be completely honest, at this point I only wanted to stop using smack enough to be able to show the court that I had changed. I didn't want to stop using altogether. The nightmares coming back, the memory of my abuse in primary school and my fear ever since resurging into my daily life was way too much to deal with when I had no coping skills that didn't involve getting shitfaced.

I made the long drive to Frankston to report to the cop-shop three times a week. I didn't want to do it in our new area; I thought that would label us locally as junkies and put us on the cops' radar. I kept this up for a few weeks but, with petrol so expensive, I just stopped going. No-one came to see me, no-one rang up to enquire why I had stopped and life just went on until the court case finally came around on the ninth of February, 2000.

BACK IN COURT (FEBRUARY 9TH 2000)

I knew about prison life from friends who'd served time, but I was worried. I didn't have any idea what I could pack to take with me, so I didn't bother to take much. The things I'd miss the most would be Carolyn, the kids, and the drugs.

I presented at the Clerk of Courts counter. Nothing was said about my failure to report to the cop-shop, so I was lucky. It could have been an extra charge. Still no idea why they never followed that up. For once, bureaucracy worked in my favour.

Carolyn was nervous, but a strange calm had settled over me. I'd resigned myself to the idea of getting locked up and had convinced myself it wouldn't be that bad. As the morning went on and cases were called, I found myself growing more and more detached from reality.

My solicitor, Simon, showed up around eleven, taking us aside and going though last-minute preparations.

"You shouldn't be called to speak until the end, just before sentencing," he said. "… but when you *are* called to speak, show the old bastard proper respect. Just say you regret the situation and have made appropriate lifestyle changes." He opened his case and got out some paperwork. "It's gonna go to a custodial sentence, but you shouldn't serve more than six months. It all depends on whether the old prick likes you or not." Simon looked up at me. "Now, you've moved from Frankston, yeah?" he asked.

"Yep," I said. "We're in Burwood now. We don't see anyone from the old days in Frankston."

"Good," he said. "I'll show that as a serious attempt to change. Have you got your methadone on track?"

"Yep. We upped our dose to eighty mill, and we're stable now."

"Good. That'll help a lot. With luck, you won't be locked up for too long."

He gathered his papers and went to get an early lunch with the police prosecutors. Carolyn and I went across to the shopping centre to get a coffee. I certainly wasn't hungry, knew I couldn't stomach anything more than that and it seemed neither could she. We were both a little stoned, having had a taste the night before and saving a small hit for the morning, as it would be my last chance for at least half a year.

We got back to the courthouse around half past one, just as the afternoon session began. After about twenty minutes, they called me into the courtroom. We filed in.

"All rise for the honourable Glen Rabbino." The clerk's voice echoed around the court, muffled by the shitty PA system. The door at the back opened, and the magistrate walked in like he had a three-foot rake up his arse and sat down behind the bench.

"You may be seated," the clerk said.

The magistrate tapped away on his computer for a moment, before looking at both the prosecutor and the defence counsel. "Gentlemen," he said. "Are we going to be here long?"

"No, your honour," the prosecutor replied. "We have a no contest plea."

The magistrate raised his brow and looked over at Simon. "Is your client pleading guilty to all charges," he asked.

"Yes, your honour," Simon replied.

"The prosecution shall read out the charges," the magistrate said.

"Yes, your honour," the prosecutor said. "The accused is charged with possession of a drug of dependence, use a drug of dependence, possess a drug of dependence with intent to traffic, and trafficking a drug of dependence. He has also been charged with possession of proceeds of crime. The accused has pled guilty to all charges."

The magistrate looked at me over the top of his wire-framed glasses. "Hmmm…" he said.

Simon got to his feet.

The magistrate looked at him. "What do you have to say on behalf of your client," the magistrate asked.

"Your honour," Simon began. "My client has led a very traumatic life. He began using drugs at a very young age, having grown up in an area where it was normalised. He has been addicted to speed for most of his life, as well as being a chronic cannabis-user."

The magistrate looked unimpressed.

Simon continued, "My client became addicted to heroin five years ago, and since then has spiralled downward and made some unwise decisions in his life." He looked over at me as he spoke. "He has managed to maintain some semblance of working, and is a trained nurse. He has worked as a carer for the disabled and has devoted a lot of time caring for others."

I'd worked on a few occasions throughout the years as a personal care attendant, but this was a big exaggeration on his part. I'd told Simon that I was registered as a nurse, and had worked for an agency for years. I neglected to mention to him that the work was few and far between. No more than ten shifts over the last five years.

"After his arrest, my client really looked at his lifestyle choices, and moved away from the area to escape the endless cycle of heroin. He has maintained a strong relationship with his partner and her children." Simon cleared his throat. "Mr Brown has also since stabilised his methadone dosage, and is now actively seeking employment."

The magistrate peered at me. "Mr Brown, have you made any attempt to get off the drugs that have, thus far, ruined your life?"

"I have, your honour," I said, standing. "As my solicitor said, I've stabilised on methadone, and have made enquiries into detox and rehab. I love my family very much, and just want to get better."

"Thank you, Mr Brown," the magistrate said. "Please sit down while I find out what options I have for sentencing." He proceeded to tap on the keyboard of the computer in front of him for another five minutes before he finally looked back to me.

"Mr Brown, you have pleaded guilty to use of heroin, and to trafficking in a drug of dependence, which is an indictable offence and punishable with level 4 imprisonment, up to 15 years," he said.

I shuddered. I didn't want to go to gaol. I felt light-headed, and the room seemed to sway a little.

The magistrate continued, "In this instance, having looked through your history with the police and the court system, and seeing no real violence or anti-societal trends other than a penchant for self-destructive behaviour, I believe that you seem a likely candidate for some level of rehabilitation, no matter that you have continued down your chosen path for over twenty years so far, and so are deserving of one final chance to do the right thing." He looked down at the screen in front of him. "As I said, you don't seem to have a history of violence. Rather, you have turned to petty theft and such to support your addiction. Without the addiction, I feel that you would not have been such an onus on society as you have been up to this point in your life."

He looked over at the prosecutor. "In the matters brought before me today, I find you guilty of all charges, and sentence you to three months imprisonment for the trafficking charge and one month imprisonment for the use of heroin, both to serve concurrently, and both wholly suspended for twelve months. On the other charges, I find them proven."

My mind raced as Simon turned to me in triumph, gesturing not to say anything until asked to speak.

"You will go to the Clerk of Courts' counter to receive the paperwork, and you *will* stay out of trouble in the future.

I suggest you find some help for your addiction, because if you come before me again, I will not be so lenient next time. Do you understand?" he asked.

"I do, your honour, and thank you," I said.

I was free. But if I offended again over the next twelve months, I'd serve at least three months before I served whatever time the new offence gave me.

I've never felt so relieved. It was only after we left the court building that it hit me just how lucky I had been.

On the way home, we stopped and scored.

Top: View of Housing Commission flats in Richmond

Bottom: The small police station set up in a walk-up flat in Richmond

THE SPLIT (2000)

Things were rough between Carolyn and me at this point. She seemed to be distancing herself from me as far as possible. We'd argue, and she'd kick me out. Carolyn was used to the pain, the emotions and the relapses of addiction, after years of using. I wasn't. I was scoring behind her back, just to feel better, even though the methadone should have been taking care of that. The thing with 'done is, you could get a further habit on top of that if you used too often. As always, for me, it was all about the 'now' and not being sick.

Carolyn either didn't suffer from the withdrawals as much as I did, or she was more used to them – I'm not sure which. Maybe I was just weak. There were so many issues between us. During the years, I'd scored without her many times and sometimes she had caught me out. She hated me doing it and took it as a betrayal. She thought using drugs without sharing was as bad as sleeping with other women.

I started staying in Rochester with Mum. Mum had no idea I'd been busted for dealing, but she knew I'd gotten in trouble, as I had to keep going to the Corrections Victoria office in Echuca, twice a week. She kept asking what had happened, and after a few weeks, I broke down and told her. We both had a cry over it, but I promised her I'd get my shit together. Easier said than done.

🖊️ 🖊️ 🖊️

Away from Melbourne, away from the extra smack on top of the methadone, I started to get sick more often. The withdrawals seemed overpowering and I had real trouble coping. The drugs, the tension, the history; they were all combining to tear Carolyn and me apart. I believed I still loved her, and I thought she still loved me. I still went to see her and the kids at least once a month, and we slept together whenever I did.

While driving back to Rochester after one visit, I found a Holden sitting beside the road with the passenger door open. I stopped to have a look.

No sign of anyone. The keys were lying on the floor. I hid them on top of one of the tyres, got back in my car and went to on to Rochy so I could grab someone to bring me back.

I got hold of a mate named Dave, and he agreed to give me a ride back to pick up the car.

We arrived, I grabbed the keys, and followed him back to Rochy, nervous all the way.

The car ran very well, a hell of a lot better than my own did at that point, and it gave me reliable transport when I most needed it. I used it to get to my community work and the sign-ins for Corrections Victoria, and I used it to go to Melbourne and score when I could afford to.

I went to markets with Mum for extra money. I bought and sold second-hand books, something I knew very well, and it helped with income. Then I discovered video piracy. It was still VHS tapes or CD-Roms back in those days, so I bought two VHS recorders and started making my own copies from pirated tapes I bought at the markets I went to.

It went well for a while.

💉 💉 💉

A month later I was staying down at Carolyn's for a couple of days. Still in the car I'd 'found', I was on my way to meet some customers to sell some videos on a nice summer's day. I had arranged to meet them at McDonald's in Richmond, so I parked there and went to call them from the public phones across the street to tell them I was waiting. I made the call only to find out they were at the other Maccas about 500 metres away, and walked back to the car, reaching into my pocket for the keys so I could drive around. Not there!

Shit!

I walked back over where I had crossed the street and checked in the still empty phone booth, but no sign of them.

Fuck!

Cursing my luck, I went back to the car to see if they had fallen to the ground. No luck there, either. I finally found them – still in the ignition and locked inside.

I went over to the shopping centre and got a coat-hanger from the dry-cleaners there. I made my way back across Church Street and started forcing the wire through the driver's side window.

I spent maybe fifteen minutes trying unsuccessfully to unlock the door when I noticed a car pull up nearby. I looked up to see it was a police divvy van.

Fuck! Somebody must have noticed me trying to break into the car and rang the cops.

I had no idea what to do, so I ended up trying to bluff my way out. If in doubt, pretend it's yours.

As the cop on the passenger side opened his door to get out, I rushed up to him. "Guys, brilliant timing. Do you have a screwdriver or a toolkit? My keys are locked in."

Looking suspicious, the cops peered into the car, but they relaxed when they saw the keys in the ignition. They must have thought I was legit once they realised I *had* locked the keys in the car. They both laughed at my stupidity and got a tool kit from their divvy van. One of them pulled out a long screwdriver and wedged it between the door and the frame of the door.

After struggling to create a gap, the other cop pushed the coat-hanger through the space and hooked it under the locking knob, flipping it up and opening the door. I was ecstatic as they put the tools back in their car, wished me a good day, and drove off.

I couldn't believe it – cops had actually helped me break into a stolen car! They hadn't bothered doing checks on me *or* the car. They hadn't even bothered asking me for ID. If they had, they'd have found I was on a suspended sentence for drugs, and investigated a little more closely.

When I finally caught up with my customers at the other Maccas around the corner on Bridge Road, I ended up selling a hundred bucks worth of movies to them. I went straight to score, and then hurried back to Carolyn's place to have a taste. Carolyn found it hilarious that the cops had helped an addict break into a stolen car.

In the end, that car only lasted another month. I ended up crashing it on my way home from Croydon Market one day. I gave the driver of the other car a fake name and address and left the scene, but I didn't make it far before the car overheated and died at the side of the road.

SEEING OTHER PEOPLE (JULY 2000)

I was staying down at Carolyn's again. Again, we'd scored the night before, and slept together.

I was still half-asleep when Carolyn came in the room and announced, "I'm having lunch with a guy I met a week or two ago at college. I hope you don't mind."

"What?" I asked.

"I think I really like this guy, and he asked me out for lunch. I'm going."

"For fuck's sake, Carolyn. I thought we'd be able to work this shit out," I yelled.

"I need something new. I need someone who won't use behind my back," she said. She grabbed her bag and left.

I ended up staying until she got home from school, but the kids were home by then and I sat there and simmered in silence. Finally, after dinner, it was too much and we started arguing again. Carolyn ended up locking herself in the bedroom, with me pummelling the door and demanding to be let in.

Carolyn's sister, Deb, was over to see the kids, and she intervened, telling me that if I didn't leave, she'd call the police.

"Get fucked, Deb. This is none of your business," I screamed.

She rang the cops.

I left.

I made my way to the church halfway up the hill, as it was a natural viewpoint to see when the cops arrived. About ten minutes later, they turned up; two cars with three or four cops in each. I don't know what Deb told them, but it must have been bad.

I could see Carolyn's front door from where I sat in the shadows, but I wanted to get closer to hear what they were saying. I made my way around the block, and snuck through a backyard to get to the shrubs that bordered the neighbour's front fence. I could hear the cops talking to Carolyn.

"And where is Geoff now, do you have any idea?"

"Nope, he left once Deborah called you guys, but he won't be far away," Carolyn said. "I know how he thinks, and he'll be hiding around here somewhere, listening to everything we're saying."

"So where do you think he'll be?"

Carolyn turned to look down the street towards where I was hidden. "He'll be close enough to hear every word we're saying. And he'll be able to see us, as well."

As she said this, I must have moved slightly to ease a rock that had been digging into me, and inadvertently rustled the bushes a little. The cops saw the motion and started towards me, so I got up on my feet and ran into the neighbour's backyard, cops yelling at me to stop. I climbed over the rear fence into a tennis court. I flew across the court, over another fence and into the small dead-end street between Carolyn's and the main road. I ran across the road as fast as I could and threw myself into another front yard. I climbed under the stairs of the veranda and hid beneath the house, making sure that I could get out the opposite end if needed. After a while, I ended up falling asleep under there. When I woke up it was just before dawn. I was cold, sore, and tired, but there were no cops around, so I went back home to find Deb gone and Carolyn asleep upstairs. I climbed into bed beside her and she snuggled in to me.

"You're such a cunt!" she said.

For the life of me I couldn't think of anything to say without starting another fight, so I rolled over to face the wall and settled down to go to sleep. About thirty seconds later Carolyn moved over and spooned me. Nothing else was said. Our relationship never stabilised after that and I ended up going back to Rochester again the next day.

Even though I was living in Rochy with Mum, I was driving down to Melbourne whenever I could, scoring when I could afford to, and then getting sick as soon as I ran out of dope.

I sold off things I owned to get money; I borrowed, begged and sometimes stole from Mum to get what I needed. I did whatever it took to feel better. It helped the withdrawals, but it didn't help anything else.

DETOX I (2000)

A round November of 2000, nine months into the suspended sentence from the dealing charges, I decided to up my methadone dose some more, stop using, and try to get stable. I wanted to go to Confest, and it was basically impossible to go anywhere for more than a day or two while on methadone. A transfer of chemists took ages to arrange, and extra doses to take-away were even harder.

I also just wanted to get my shit together.

I had been dropping cautiously over the last six months, and was down to forty milligrams of methodone a day, so I made an appointment to go see my doctor. I ended up raising the dose to fifty-five milligrams and that helped me feel more comfortable. I still wasn't sleeping well, and I felt crappy at night, but during the day it was better. After a week, I stabilised. No withdrawal symptoms apart from trouble staying asleep overnight.

I settled down for a while, getting my daily dose of 'done – travelling thirty clicks to the chemist in Echuca every day to pick it up. That was bad enough, but I still went down to Melbourne to score at least once a fortnight. Things had to change. I researched the various detox services that were offered, and decided that Wellington House, the detox unit attached to the Box Hill Hospital, offered the best residential service I could find. The place was new and very nice, the medication regime seemed to cover all the symptoms I was likely to suffer, and it was close to Carolyn's place so she could visit me if she chose.

A requirement of Wellington House was that you needed to be a resident of the surrounding area. Living in rural Victoria, my options were limited; they wouldn't take me. I overcame this by telling them, with her permission, that I lived with Carolyn, so I had an address in Box Hill.

I went down for an interview and assessment in late December, and they judged me as suitable for treatment. I was booked in to attend the first week of the New Year.

I went home and got everything ready. I packed a portable CD player, my CDs, a guitar, a journal notebook and some pads to write in. I was excited. I started to lower my dose of methadone again, to get to a stage where quitting would be easier.

The time sped by and, in the first week of January I drove down to stay at Carolyn's place the night before I was due to check in. We scored that night, my last chance for a taste, or so I thought.

After we got stoned, Carolyn told me about a new guy she'd met — Colin — and how she liked him. I was too stoned and too worried about going into detox to take it in. I just assumed that once I had gone through the detox program, we'd be together again. That we'd live happy ever after in a land of unicorns and fairy floss, even though I wanted to stop using and that is not possible while in a relationship with another user.

WELLINGTON HOUSE (JANUARY 2001)

The next morning, Carolyn came with me to the detox unit. We said goodbye, I thanked her for looking after my car while I was inside, and said it was fine for her to use the vehicle so long as she put petrol in and left the key hidden in a pre-arranged place in her backyard in case she wasn't home when I got through.

I was ushered inside and all my bags were searched to ensure I wasn't trying to smuggle in drugs. It may seem silly to be trying to take drugs into detox, but many addicts go in for their parents, their partners, or for the court system, so they try to get the drugs they still crave into the unit with them.

All the rooms were clean and new, painted in pastel colours that were designed to be soothing. When I arrived, a worker led me past a kitchen and a nurse's station, along a corridor, and finally to my room for the next two weeks. It was all single room accommodation, to make it harder for the suffering junkies to disturb each other's precarious hold on sleep.

There were around ten other clients here. There were two wings to the building, each holding five single bedrooms. I quickly unpacked my things and went out to the common room to meet the other residents. Out of all of them, I can only clearly remember one.

Fiona – Fee – was short, blonde and cute. She was also damaged goods, just how I liked my girls. I found out later that, raped and abused as a child, she'd drifted fast into the world of drugs, starting with speed and progressing quickly to heroin. She'd ended up selling her body for years to pay for her habit; it was the only life she knew.

I had a crush on her from day one.

In detox, it's not unusual to latch onto someone; a sort of support-network-by-proxy, I guess. It makes it easier to get through if you have someone to focus on outside of yourself. I found Fee.

Detox was great. I was in there to get off the methadone, fooling myself into thinking it would be easy to get off the opiates altogether. I planned to get off 'done and never touch heroin again. Methadone is a substitute for smack, and if I managed to get off that, I wouldn't need smack, either. The opiate addiction would be gone.

What I didn't take into account is that I was in no shape mentally to kick anything. Sure, I did fine while in the unit, but they medicate you there to ensure you don't suffer from any physical withdrawal symptoms. I didn't feel a thing: I slept like a baby, ate well, felt good in every way. I was worried about things with Carolyn, but I had fooled myself into thinking that would be fine as well.

Stupid me.

I spent time talking to Fee, playing guitar, reading, and socialising with the others.

I was on forty milligrams of 'done a day when I went in. I was reducing down to zero in the span of fourteen days, so the doctors worked out a reduction timetable that got me there with as little discomfort as possible. The normal detox drugs are dispensed on-site by the nurses, but for people like me on a methadone reduction plan, it was necessary to be walked to the Box Hill Hospital, around the corner in Arnold St, and dosed over there by a doctor each day.

About six days into the program, I went over to the hospital to get my daily dose. I had it, but it seemed at the time more than it should be. It seems that the hospital, in their infinite wisdom and oversight, had given me fifteen millilitres rather than fifteen milligrams. Fifteen mills of the liquid methadone is around seventy-five milligrams of drug, five times what I was actually meant to receive. Needless to say, they were worried.

They made me sit at the hospital, monitored every half an hour by bored nurses in case I overdosed. I still had enough of a tolerance that it barely staggered me at all. I certainly didn't feel stoned; I was just a little tired and ended up having a nap when I finally went back to the unit. I don't know if that fucked up my detox program or not, but I can guarantee that I wasn't ready to get clean at that point anyway.

I spent the days talking, smoking and undergoing therapeutic programs involving relaxation techniques, crisis identification and how to cope with cravings. At night we watched movies or just sat outside and smoked cigarettes and talked for hours. Twice we went to local meetings of Narcotics Anonymous. Overall, detox seemed a waste of time for three quarters of the clients. They were in for all the wrong reasons – me included.

Fee left early, about four days before I was due for release, and she promised to keep in touch. We'd spent a bit of time together, and I really liked her. For all the wrong reasons.

While I was in treatment, Colin and Carolyn became close, to the point where two days before I was due to finish the fourteen-day program, she called to tell me that we were over and that she was now with Colin. I could pick up my car when I was finished, but that was it. Game over.

I hung up the phone and cursed all the way to my room, slamming the door behind me. Within a minute, one of the counsellors knocked and asked if anything was the matter. I don't know if I told her anything, it's all foggy, but they left me alone after that. I eventually went out back for a cigarette, and the other clients were sympathetic ears when I told them what had happened. One of them had smuggled in some weed, but we couldn't just fill a cigarette tube with dope and sit outside smoking it, so eventually one of us came up with the bright idea of making an apple pipe. The idea is to make a tunnel through the centre of the apple. A silver foil cone with pinholes in it is placed over one hole, dope is put in the cone and then you suck through the other hole as you light the dope. *Voila.*

One of the workers came out around 8pm, just as I was about to light up, but I saw her coming through the glass door and pretended to munch on the apple.

We didn't get caught, we all got stoned, and I went to bed.

The time I spent in Wellington House was comfortable and easy. They used a mix of medications to ease the withdrawal for opiate reduction, typically clonidine, Valium, ibuprofen, Stemetil, and Imodium. A smorgasbord of drugs to counter all the effects of coming off the gear. I barely felt any withdrawal, so it was certainly working for me.

The next morning, around eight o'clock, I got another phone call.

"Hello," I said.

"Geoff? It's Fee. I'm really sick and I can't take it anymore. I don't want to do anything stupid. Can you help me out?" she asked.

"What can I do? I'm here for two more days," I said. "Can't you get on the 'done?"

"I can't wait. I've been sick since I got out of there. I need something now." She started to cry.

"Fee, just go and see a doctor," I said.

"I can't," she answered. "I can't wait that long. Can't you get me some cash?" she asked.

"How can I do that, Fee? Like I said, I'm here for another two days." I felt helpless. I knew what it was like to suffer through withdrawals, but at the same time I must have known I was just being conned again. "Isn't there anyone else you can ask?"

"I've got no-one except you," she sobbed.

"Call me back in ten minutes, okay?" I said.

"All right" she said, "but if you can't help me, I'm going to go see work to get some cash."

"Work?" I queried.

"You know what I mean. I'll go to St Kilda and fuck someone who's willing to pay for me," she said.

"Look, just don't do anything stupid. Let me work out what I can do. Call me back in five minutes, okay?"

"Sure, Geoff. I'll talk to you in a bit. And thanks."

I rang Mum as soon as Fee hung up.

"Hi Mum," I said. "How are you?"

"I'm good.," she said. "How are you going?"

"I'm great," I said. "Look, I need some money to pay for the final stage of treatment."

She sighed. "How much?"

"Um... two hundred should cover it, and it'll give me petrol money to travel home when I get out," I said.

"All right," she said. "When do you need it by?"

"I'm supposed to go to see the doctor in an hour, so I'll need it straight away," I lied.

"Okay," she said. "I'll go down to the bank now."

"Thanks," I said. "I have to go now, so I'll talk to you later."

Against everything I should be doing, I had decided that enough was enough, and I'd leave to be with Fee so I could score as well. Thinking about it had made me edgy, and I really wanted a hit. I'm not sure if I was conned by Fee to be her knight in shining armour, conned by myself with an excuse to fail, or a mixture of both.

Five minutes later, Fee rang back.

"I've organised some cash, so I'll check out of here and we can go score," I said.

"Thank you so much," she said, suddenly brighter than she had been the previous phone call. "Where can I meet you?"

"Get to Richmond, and I'll meet you out front of the train station as soon as I can get there."

"You're awesome," she said. "See you soon."

"You too, Fee" I said. "Just make sure you meet me there."

I hung up.

I'd packed within fifteen minutes, then took my bags and guitar up to the office. The case-workers weren't happy with the news that I was checking out, but it was a voluntary unit – we were all there of our own free will, to a greater or lesser degree.

I left detox and went up to Carolyn's place where I had left my car. She wasn't there, so I grabbed the key from the backyard and left to meet Fiona.

After I'd picked her up, Fee talked non-stop.

"So, how much are we getting?" she asked.

"I've got two hundred, so we can grab half a gram and I'll still have some cash left over for food and something to drink." I said.

"Do you think that'll be enough?" she asked. I should have recognised the signs of her infatuation with using me. I should have been more careful here, but as usual, I was desperate for acceptance and desperate to love and be loved in return. I just hadn't worked out it could never be with another junkie.

"Geez, Fee. Neither of us have used since we went into detox, so we need to be careful not to OD."

"I guess you're right... " she said.

By the time we got to Victoria Street, we were both anxious, with sweat beginning to stream down our faces. We were both fidgety as well, although with the driving at least I had something to take my mind off the wait.

We parked the car and walked down the street, looking for dealers I knew rather than risking buying from someone unknown and getting ripped off. Some things changed in Richmond's heroin scene, but other things stayed the same.

Soon enough, I found Nam, an Asian dealer I knew well. He had great gear in good sizes, so I bought half a gram from him and we went back to the car for a taste.

This became standard every day for a week, begging, borrowing or stealing to raise the cash to score. Soon enough, I worked out I was being used by Fee to cover her habit. In exchange, we had sex every night, so I suppose she thought of it as barter. After a week of this, I realised we were sinking rapidly, so I told Fee that I'd decided to go back to Rochester.

"What about us?" she asked.

"What us?" I said. "We're getting further and further in the shit. I want to stop using. That's why I was in detox in the first place."

"What about me, then?" she said.

"Can't you go on the methadone?" I asked.

"I don't want to go on the 'done," she said. "I want to get smashed."

"How are you gonna stop using without 'done?" I asked.

"I don't *want* to stop using!"

"You should," I said, "because it's gonna kill you one of these days."

"Fuck, Geoff. I don't need you preaching to me. It's not like you can talk. You're just as fucked as I am." She stormed out of the car and ran off.

I already had a habit at least as large as before I went in, so I just went home and back on the methadone program.

CAUGHT AGAIN (2001)

I t was halfway through 2001, and I was down in Melbourne staying with Carolyn yet again. Our relationship was strange, just like most of my relationships while I was fucked up; we weren't really together, but we still saw each other a lot. We'd use, we'd fight, I'd leave, and a month later she'd call me or I'd call her, and we'd do it all over again. Friends without benefits. Junkie relationship.

I was sick, as I always missed doses of 'done when I went down, and needed some cash to score. I stepped out of the shower at her place, towelled myself dry and got dressed in record time. I was sick, shaking and sweating. I needed to source some cash and get on for both of us.

I told Carolyn I'd be back by lunchtime with some gear and drove to the K-Mart at Burwood East. I was wearing a baggy t-shirt with a collared shirt over the top. This ensemble helped to cover up the bulges under my arms and down the front of my pants. I usually stole to order for book-shop owners, or else just took the latest releases by big name authors. I made my way to the book department and started checking out the New Release section. I grabbed two large hardcover books and stuffed them under my left armpit. I'd get ten bucks each for them.

I grabbed another couple and jammed them into the front of my jeans. I checked that the bulge wasn't too noticeable. Two more went under my right arm. I went back out the front exit and made my way down to the car, stashed the books and covered them with a blanket. Sixty dollars, as quick as that.

I made two more trips without a problem. On the fourth trip, I grabbed a couple of new street directories, as I knew someone who'd buy them for fifteen bucks each. I made my way out the front exit this time but, within twenty yards of the door, I was grabbed from behind.

"Excuse me, sir. Would you mind accompanying us back to the store, please?" It was two security guards. I debated just dropping the books and running, but decided against it. I just didn't have the energy, and I didn't want to escalate the situation.

"What's up, guys? I just wanna get home, and I don't have time for this," I said.

"Sir, just accompany us back into the store. We don't want any trouble," one said to me while they moved in on each side of me, ready to grab if I tried to do a runner.

They led me back inside and through to one of the offices at the back of the store.

"I take it you want these back?" I asked as I pulled the Melways out from under my shirt and plonked them onto the desk.

"That would be good, sir," the guard said. The other had left once I was inside the office, obviously satisfied that I wasn't going to give them any trouble.

He made a call to the local police station letting them know they'd arrested a shoplifter.

He opened a drawer and pulled out a sheet of paper and started to fill it out. He ignored me as we both waited for the cops to arrive. Ten minutes later, the door opened and two uniformed officers walked in.

"What's the story, Paul?" one cop asked the guard.

"We watched this guy attempting to steal some books from the store We grabbed him once he was outside."

The cop turned to me. "Mate, you are now under arrest on suspicion of theft. We'll take you back to the station where you'll be interviewed in relation to the matter. Any questions?"

"Nope," I said. "Let's get this over with." I was glad I was finished with the suspended sentence, but I also knew I likely wouldn't get any free chances this time. I'd be lucky to make bail. It sure looked like I was in for a bad few days as the withdrawals kicked in.

The two cops took a step forward. "We need to search you before we go anywhere. Have you got any other stolen goods on you?"

"Nope," I replied truthfully. They were all out in the car, on the back floor and covered with a blanket.

"Have you got any weapons or sharp objects on you?" he asked.

"Nope," I said again.

The senior constable moved forward and asked me to stand up. I did so, and he searched my clothing and pockets but found nothing. Lucky they had no idea that I had nearly two hundred bucks worth of books out in the car, along with syringes and the rest of my gear I needed to shoot up with. I was cuffed and taken away.

Within minutes of arriving at Nunawading police station, I was put in an interview room and the hand-cuffs were removed. I was left on my own while they went off to do all the usual paperwork. I was freaking, worried that I'd start to go into withdrawal soon. I didn't want to stay in the cells until I went to court, but it seemed a certainty.

It took nearly two hours to complete the whole process, and because of my record, I assumed I'd be locked up without bail. To my surprise, I was let go just after lunch.

I immediately made my way back to the car and drove to the bookshop. I ended up making a hundred and eighty bucks from the books, and went to score. I stayed with Carolyn for another two days, until my payday, and scored a gram of smack to take back to Rochester with me.

I failed to notice that stealing was becoming more natural to me than it ever had before. I felt it was justified by my illness; the sicker I felt, the less I thought about it.

DETOX II (2001-02)

By now, Carolyn had gotten pretty serious with Colin. He'd moved into her place in Burwood, and that part of my life was over. I stayed in Rochester most of the time after fucking up my detox in Box Hill, still on the methadone program for another twelve months, but I wasn't happy. I decided I wanted to try to clean up again a year after the first attempt. How much longer could I live the life of a useless junkie? I was in my thirties, for fuck's sake.

I was also sick of driving two hours each day, of being tied to a pharmacy by chemical chains, so I reduced to ten milligrams daily and through my doctor at the community health centre, booked in at DePaul House, a city detox-unit connected to St Vincent's Hospital and run by the non-government organisation St Vincent de Paul Society.

DePaul House was in an old pub in Fitzroy Street, just off Victoria Street near the CBD. It was dark and dingy, with narrow halls and doorways and communal rooms shared by five or six sick addicts.

The medication regime there was, to say the least, missing a lot of what was provided at Wellington House. It left me suffering from withdrawal symptoms that were bearable during the day but made the night-time hours a living hell. No sleep combined with aching legs and back made for a terrible stay of ten days. I never really clicked with any of the other people in there for detox, not like I did at Box Hill. That was good in the sense that I wouldn't allow someone else to hijack my recovery the way I did with Fiona, but it does help to be able to talk to someone. To gain a sense of solidarity in suffering.

I'll never forget the nights with the endless hours of withdrawal. The vain pleading with the workers for more sleep meds. The cramps and the sweats followed immediately by chills through my whole body.

It was a week spent in hell, but I stuck it out.

The morning I was released happened to be my payday as well, and since I was still feeling sick, I hopped on a tram that took me straight to Richmond to score. I didn't care that I'd just struggled for a week to get off opiates; I just wanted to feel better. For me, it was all about instant-gratification. It was easy to look at the long-term when I was stoned, but as soon as I got sick, I didn't care about the future – I just wanted to feel better. Like all junkies, I operated in the 'now'.

I still wonder if, with a better medication regime and less suffering during my stay, I would have made the same decisions that particular time.

With heroin dealers literally a thousand metres from the front door the day I was released, I was stoned within thirty minutes of getting out. It was the best I'd felt in nearly two weeks, and I scored a gram to take back with me. I spent everything I had, except enough for a coffee and train-fare. I used every day for a week, and when I ran out of stuff I went straight to the doctor and ended up on the methadone program again.

Maybe it'd be third time lucky, but I was beginning to doubt I would ever get free of opiates. It was a harder battle than I'd thought. They say as long as you keep trying, you haven't failed. I still wanted to get clean, and I kept trying. I stabilised – again – on the methadone, thirty milligrams daily, and started reducing yet again.

The methadone doctor I was seeing was constantly at me to stay on the program for life.

"You know you shouldn't even consider going off your dose, don't you?" he always asked me, whenever I wanted to reduce. A lot of prescribing doctors are of the mind that addicts are broken, and can never be repaired. That they need medicating until the day they die, or else they will just go back to old habits no matter what.

In the end, he refused to lower my dosage, but I knew my rights and I organised with the chemist to lower the dose every two weeks. The doctors have to give you permission to raise the dose, but not to lower it.

DETOX III (2002-03)

Twelve months later, I was ready to try again. It seemed an annual thing for me at this point. To get sick of being on 'done and to try to find a way to get opiate-free, yet at the same time driving to Melbourne on occasion to score. I was finding more and more of my childhood memories resurfacing as I lowered my medication dose. I was still determined to be free of the chains of addiction. I wanted some sort of life.

By this point, I had a desktop computer, and was starting to foster a friendship base in online chat rooms dedicated to the reading, writing, and collecting of horror books. My favourite genre since I was a teenager, the following for horror online through a site called Horror Mall was large and active. For once I had a place I could talk to people that didn't take drugs. People who lived normal lives, and didn't judge me based on anything but what I read and said online. It certainly helped me feel more normal than I had for most of my life. A whole new feeling of acceptance that didn't rest on how many drugs I could take and supply, on how 'connected' I was to suppliers, or to how much cash I had. I had suddenly found a group that cared what I had to say for no reason other than discovery of new opinions, and excitement around a common interest in horror literature.

Strengthened and with a more positive outlook, I did some research on various places. I found I couldn't get back into Wellington House without a local address and I had no desire to ever see DePaul House again. I settled on a place in Abbotsford run by the Salvation Army, who accepted people from all over the state.

The Bridge Detox Centre, on Victoria Crescent near Gipps Street, was a fantastic place.

I ended up in a private room, and the staff were a wonderful group of people. They supported me when I needed it, but left me alone when I didn't. A lot seemed to be streetwise, so I had an idea they were ex-users themselves, but they would never open up about their own past.

The Bridge took both genders in, and it had separate areas for the guys and girls. To get to the girls' area, you had to go past the front desk, where there was always a staff-member on duty. Any physical contact was against the rules. Out the front, there were seats and a covered area for smoking. Addicts tend to smoke a lot in detox.

The Bridge offered a ten-day medicated program that focused on therapy and group sessions. The medication regime worked well, unlike DePaul House, and it was a time that could be spent coming off drugs without any real discomfort, although some complained of the aches and pains of withdrawal. I tend to think people got what they expected to get. Those who didn't really want to be there, who expected to suffer, did suffer. I sure as hell felt good, though.

Between the Valium and the sleeping tablets, as well as the clonidine to ease the symptoms, I always felt more normal in most detox units than I did outside. I really thought this time would make the difference. I felt strong while I went through the week-and-a-half, and by the time I got to the eighth day, my meds had been dropped to basically some ibuprofen for the aches and pains and that was all. I didn't need sleepers to drop off, nor did I need the Valium for the anxiety of being drug-free. At least until the minute I walked out the gate, happy and proud to have made it through, and sure I was now king of the world.

I scored within ten minutes of my check-out. The residential unit is about five hundred metres from 'Heroin Central' in Richmond, which I had to walk through to get the train home, and I had a Centrelink payment in my bank account. It's like a switch flicks over to 'stupid' as soon as I'm loose in Melbourne with money. I don't think of anything but the rush of the taste. Once I'm stoned, I regret it, but up until then, I just concentrate on getting high.

I walked towards North Richmond train station, determined to stay straight and narrow, to make the right choice for once in a lifetime of wrong ones.

In the distance I could see the Housing Commission flats. I could smell the heroin from here. I knew there were at least ten or twenty dealers holding gear between me and the train, and my gut just went empty and black, and I knew what would happen before I even made up my mind that it didn't matter. Just once more. Just one more taste to say goodbye to the gear. Just one more to excuse to myself and... and then I suddenly didn't care. All I cared about was feeling the rush as I slid the needle into my arm and pressed the plunger and the drug would hit my brain. There would be time for guilt and recriminations later, but for now all I cared about was a taste. Just one more.

It's bittersweet that the detox units are almost always near the areas where drugs are rife. It helps for access for the street addicts, but makes temptation too easy when you leave. I went back to live with Mum, with a half-gram in my pocket. It was time for the methadone again. No gain at all, but there's always next time. At least, that's what I told myself.

RICHARD, AMBA AND GLENN

I met Richard and Naomie at the methadone clinic. They seemed to be good people. Richard sold weed and I needed somewhere to score in Rochester, as it was too expensive to drive to Echuca every time I wanted to get on. They lived less than a kilometre from my place and he always had nice dope.

It worked well and we became friends, or so I thought. A year or so later, he was starting to fuck up on drugs, using more and more speed, although I had no idea just how far he would fall. From what I know now, after he lost most of his money on drugs he blamed his fiancée Naomie for ripping him off thousands of dollars, and costing him the two-bedroom unit he was buying at the time. Now I tend more toward thinking he did that all to himself.

Back then, I believed him, taking him at his word.

When he finally split with her, he had to move out of the unit, having defaulted on the payments. He ended up sharing with me for a month or two, working at a vineyard just over the border in Moama.

After a month of staying at Mum's house, he was granted a cheap house in Echuca by the Housing Commission.

He had another ex in Echuca, and a younger son with her. In truth, Richard was more interested in hard drugs and teenage girls than in being a father. He was still dealing weed in Echuca, but started using more and more speed, eventually selling that as well, although the quality was most often pretty average. I think he was just too greedy, cutting whatever he got to make more money, but at the same time, speed that made it out of the city and into regional area was usually crap anyway. I was using more and more speed hanging with him, and it was starting to show. I lost weight and had a continual speed-buzz, not sleeping well except when I went to Melbourne and scored some smack.

Richard and I were the best of mates. I spent a lot of time with him at his place, and it became second-nature to drive up to Echuca and spend three days at a time, smoking, playing console games, and shooting speed when we could afford to.

I got a job at the Moama paintball place, setting up and guiding tours, and then cleaning all the equipment up at the end of the day. It was long hours and hard work, especially in the hottest and coldest months, but I enjoyed it. I could use my imagination to tell the story for each game field, whether terrorists to kill or hostages to rescue, and I felt like I had some level of respect. That lasted about a year before I moved once again.

I met another couple at the clinic too: Amba and Glenn.

An unusual couple as Amba was a heroin addict, but Glenn didn't do any drugs at all. Hell, didn't even smoke cigarettes.

Usually, non-druggies didn't want relationships with addicts, and if they did, the relationships didn't last very long, but Glenn was a natural for the darker side of society, criminally-minded with a love of guns and cash, as well as being totally infatuated and obsessed with Amba, which I could understand. She was an attractive girl, seven years his junior, with beautiful features and a nice figure. They ended up moving to Melbourne not long after I met them, and I made the mistake of going along with them, at their invitation.

Glenn worked as a watchmaker in the city, leaving Amba and myself to go on mad missions to raise money: beg or borrow from relatives or friends, steal from the bigger stores and sell stuff at the pawn shops, whatever it took to get on. I often rang Mum with some lame excuse of why I needed money. This recurring theme is, and always will be, one of the major shameful things of my life.

We were living in St Albans in the outer west, so we scored around Footscray, the western suburbs Mecca for addicts and dealers.

It didn't take us long to find a reasonable supplier who always had gear and carried a mobile phone. He was a typical dealer for that era, young and addicted. He supported his own habit by dealing to others on the street.

Tran was one of the more straight-looking street-addicts. He at least maintained a facade of civility, making a cursory attempt to maintain a level of personal hygiene and dress that didn't make him stand out to the cops too much. Very much a businessman in the world of capitalist drug supply. Dealers had it really hard and really easy at the same time. There was the constant risk of arrest and gaol, but on the flip-side, no advertising, just turning up; no sales-pitch, just supply and all the demand you could ever ask for. Drugs, the perfect consumerism. How could anyone say it wasn't democratic to need a fix?

He was down the street early every day, usually near the marketplace just north of the train station, attempting to mingle with the early shoppers. I grabbed some deals from him and we went back to Amba's car to fix up our taste.

That became routine.

Amba and I used every day for about three months before we both rang the same day to arrange detox at The Bridge. Normally friends wouldn't be placed in at the same time where possible, but they could never police that, as most junkies from the same suburb knew each other.

The check-in was the same. The routine was the same. The medications were the same. We went through a week of slowly reducing our meds with the help of the doctor and counsellors, and things were going great.

Then a new guy named Sean, only three days into his detox, pulled a few of us aside and said he wanted to score. He could make a call and arrange to get heroin and some fits delivered, and wanted people to put in cash so they could get a larger amount. Amba and I quickly agreed, finding fifty dollars each.

Just after dark, Sean collected our money and went to the side fence where there was a walkway. He passed the money to a hand that appeared, grabbed the smack that was passed back, then we split it between us and went off to our rooms to have a taste.

Soon enough, we were all lolling around in the common room or letting our cigarettes burn away to ash on the outside seating. On the nod and feeling good.

It took the workers on duty less than five minutes to work out that something was up. They weren't stupid, and like I'd noticed the first visit, a lot of them seemed to have a pretty good handle on the lifestyle, as though they'd lived it rather than just learning about it from books.

Sure enough, the whole unit was asked to do a piss-test the next morning. I was crafty enough to grab a bit of lemon cordial and mix it with warm water to approximate the colour of piss. I never found out if I passed or failed, as Amba and I finished our program the next day anyway, but I bet if they'd tested for sugar levels it would've freaked them out.

Once we finished detox, we stayed straight until my payday. I suggested we have a taste 'for old time's sake'. It took another week until we were back using every day. Same old excuse, same old slipping backwards.

Just one more.

Just one.

Glenn was pissed we'd fucked up, but I guess he'd had enough experience dealing with Amba's addiction he knew the routine and was just glad we were still trying.

A few months later, we tried again. A doctor I knew about in Thornbury prescribed home-detox drugs, so we thought we'd give that a go this time, rather than checking into residential detox. We went and saw him, and he pre-scribed us enough Valium and clonidine for two weeks.

We sat at home for most of those days, off our heads, feeling quite good, and not worrying about scoring. The Valium high was pretty good. I look back now and thank god I never got hooked on that stuff. From what I hear, it's much harder to break that habit than it is to stop using smack.

Eventually we got to the end of the prescription stuff, and started to think about other drugs. It's usually a case of 'oh, I can use once or twice and enjoy it without getting back on the shit'. Addicts can justify anything to get another hit. And believe me, we do.

Soon enough we were back to scoring every few days, then every second, which quickly became every day. Finally, we got to a day with no cash and started to get sick by lunch. I called Mum and begged for money. I told her I had court fines to pay so I wouldn't be locked up. She seemed to believe me, and she deposited the money in about an hour.

We went to Footscray and scored a half gram between us. Our tolerance had dropped, and we got smashed on such a big score. This is what usually kills addicts. They reduce their intake for whatever reason: gaol, detox, no smack, or just low-quality stuff. Then the good stuff hits the streets again, and they score and inject the same amount they've always used. Instant overdose. We were lucky that day. Neither of us died.

Within two weeks, we were both back on methadone again. A great big circle. The whole thing just seemed too much, too big a hurdle to be able to overcome without stronger self-control. We were both on fifteen milligrams at the time, a low dose, but if we were to start using again it would creep up very quickly. At this point, the lifestyle was getting to me. Amba had Glenn, but I had no-one, or so it seemed, so I decided to go back to stay with Mum in Rochester. At this point, she was spending more time staying with a friend who'd just lost her husband, and I had the house to myself.

Nothing much changed. I was going to Melbourne and scoring at least once a week at first, then it became more and more often until I was going every second day. Same old shit for the next two years.

TRYING AGAIN (2005)

Carolyn and I had stayed in touch through all this, with me mistaking co-dependence and a desire to be loved for friendship. Even though she was with Colin, we both believed we were best friends. I went down to visit – and use smack – with them both at least once a month. Colin didn't like it, but she gave him little choice. It was 2005 and her son Julian was having difficulties at school. After being kicked out of two schools for bad behaviour, he was going to be sent to a school for kids who were hard to control. Carolyn didn't want this so I came up with an alternative.

Julian moved up to Rochester with me, and went to Rochester Secondary College, a school with a reputation for helping troubled kids adjust.

While he stayed with me, I still scored every few days, either travelling down while he was at school or taking him along for the drive.

It seemed I'd never change. When I began the whole detox thing, I thought I saw a light at the end of the tunnel. But, after all the failures, I began to sink into a depression, thinking it was all hopeless. I nearly gave up. I felt like necking myself, but never found the determination to fully carry it out.

Then came the day I was down in Melbourne scoring with Carolyn. Colin was at work, and we were in Richmond. I'd just scored in a toilet block from a guy who was selling from the pool of vomit on the floor. Carolyn followed me in for a taste once I had the gear.

We ended up sitting in the park, and I realised just how much I hated myself for being so weak. I lay there, looking up at the sky, full of self-doubt and loathing.

All sorts of thoughts went through my head that day as we sat in the sun, stoned out of our brains.

I wondered where I was going, I wondered about the wisdom of wanting to be with Carolyn, I wondered if I could ever get off this shit, this drug, this death sentence. I knew I was worthless, still, but surely I was worth more than this? Mum still thought so. Out of all the people in my life, she'd never given up on me. Never.

I thought about the things I had done over the years: all the stealing; all the dealing; all the lying and all the deception.

I felt a change come over me.

I knew it couldn't continue, I couldn't go on this way. No more. I didn't know how, but this time I knew it had to happen. I had to do it now.

No more lying, no more wheeling and dealing. I'd put all those I cared about through the wringer, both emotionally and financially. I had to make a change, and I had to get out of this lifestyle.

I had to break the cycle.

BUPE (LATE 2005)

Buprenorphine – 'Bupe' – was first introduced in Britain as a treatment for acute and chronic pain in the 1980s. Nearly twenty years later, it was approved in the US for use in addiction treatment, and it arrived in Australia soon after.

After talking to my doctor, I decided to swap to this treatment. I was on forty milligrams of methadone at the time, at least ten mills too high to comfortably swap over.

I went on a quick reduction schedule and got down to twenty-five mills of 'done. I changed over, feeling a bit sick for a few days but nothing too bad.

One of the real advantages of the new treatment was that it reduced the effectiveness of any heroin I tried to use. I either didn't feel it very much, or didn't feel it at all. It became pointless to travel all the way to Melbourne to score, so I stopped using IV drugs regularly for the first time in twenty-two years.

I began to see it was possible to live a life without heroin; a way to get out of the never-ending cycle I'd been in for so many years.

If I wanted to have a taste, I needed to miss the Bupe for at least two days. I did this on occasion, but not enough to say I was still a regular user. It was the best I'd done for most of my life. Then I worked out you could inject the stuff.

The chemist dispensed it as a powder taken under the tongue, but I began to divert it; trying to keep the powder from dissolving by drying my mouth with tissues before I entered the pharmacy and then scraping it out into a spoon. Then I would go out to the parking lot and mix it up to have a taste. I didn't see that this was just another way to fuck up the treatment. I still consciously thought I was doing well. It's amazing how we can fool ourselves if we just try a little.

I was on eight milligrams of Bupe to start with, equal to twenty-four millilitres of methadone. I reduced yet again over a six-month period and got back down to two milligrams.

I was on such a small dose, I decided to try detox again. I felt embarrassed knowing that the dirty urine-test results would be in my file at The Bridge, but I went back down to Melbourne a week later, determined to give it another try.

This was the same as all the other times I'd admitted myself, with one exception. I'd organised to go straight on from detox to a rehabilitation unit in the outer east called The Basin. It was a four-month program on a working dairy farm at the foot of Mt Dandenong, and was a well-respected facility run as part of The Bridge program. I'd never tried rehab after detox before. I'd never thought I needed it. Now, I knew I had to try something different. I hoped that this time would be the habit-breaker.

REHAB (2006)

I have always loved going into detox. I guess it was the safety net of the medications and the passing over of control to the doctors and counsellors, but I loved the social side as well. It was always a great feeling of inclusion, sitting around with all the other addicts and alcoholics, understanding them, empathising with them and talking for hours about how we'd all get better. Talking positive as much for ourselves as for our listeners. Convincing ourselves that this time would be different, this time we'd make it through. The ones who wanted to make it, that is. There are always different desires in these settings.

The ones who really want to get off the gear tend to congregate together while the others, the ones who are only in for a break from the lifestyle or for a court case or to get their kids back, they tend to sit apart and plot their scams for the day they get out. A kind of junkie networking service. I had done the same thing many times, unable to see my mistake.

During my stay, the second-last day I think, my pay was deposited in my bank. I had scored just before I arrived at the unit, and I still had the syringe I'd smuggled into the unit in my underpants.

Once more won't hurt. Just for old-time's sake.

Setting myself up for failure without even realising it, same as usual. It's this sort of self-justification that is always my downfall. Even though I thought I was worthless, I also thought I was above what happened to others. Somehow, I was better. A weird dichotomy in the way I think.

I took a book outside to pretend I was reading, went around the corner of the building and jumped the fence. I walked to Victoria Street as quickly as I could. I scored within a few minutes and walked back to the unit again. As I'd pointed out before, The Bridge was only five hundred metres away from the local smack circuit.

I jumped back over the fence and got upstairs without anyone being the wiser. I spent my last night in detox stoned.

The next day, the bus picked me up to take me to the rehab site. I suffered for my mistake in rehab, unable to sleep and stricken with heavy cramping and diarrhoea for the two nights I stayed.

The Basin was a working farm. People arrived to start a four-month programme, and the first night they were toured around and shown how it worked. The accommodation was shared, with recently-opened accommodation units housing about four people with shared facilities. The place was really nice. Everyone ate together at the same times, and everyone worked from their second or third day on site, depending on their ability.

The Basin ran through three stages: the first month is orientation, and getting used to the rehabilitation process. Then the next two months would be focused on the self-healing and recovery process through work, personal responsibility, and group workshops designed to promote recovery, self-actualisation, coping mechanisms to prevent relapse, and a new faith in your own ability to become a good citizen and contribute to your own future. The final four weeks are based around a transition from supported recovery to a self-reliant skill-based way of life that no longer included drugs.

There was a strong push towards religion and the twelve-step programs, which I'd never really liked, as they focused on admitting we were helpless to ever make our own change, rather pushing us towards looking for an external power to help. For me, it seemed a hypocritical option when every other taught skill seemed to suggest self-reliance.

On the third day, I packed my bags and asked for the remainder of the fortnight's rent I'd paid to be refunded pro-rata. I'd just been too sick, and I knew the constant push to religion would wear thin with me very soon. That would never be my way out.

I took the cash, caught the train to Richmond, and scored. It took nearly three hours to get there from The Basin, but it felt like thirty hours. I spewed up at least three times on the train, and nearly chucked all over the dealer I scored from.

When I finally had a whack, it was the greatest relief I had ever felt in my long, drug-addled life. I knew it was both wrong and stupid, but addicts look at the now. As usual, I caught the bus back up to Rochy and went back on the Bupe.

When I got back to Rochester, I started spending more and more time with Richard again. We were using speed and smoking dope as much as we could, and using smack every now and then when we could get to Melbourne.

This went on for about a year. It could have gone on a lot longer but Richard ended up getting kicked out of his house. He owed money to half of Echuca, and the other half hated him without being owed anything. I also found out he was supplying young teenage girls with drugs in exchange for sex. He really was a dirty piece of shit. I just didn't know it.

When I'd first met him, he had a quiet intelligence and charm that the drugs – mostly speed – took away from him. Either that or he was always that-way-inclined, and just hid it well. I tend to think the latter applies. I lost contact with him after that until I heard he had been gaoled for eight years for kidnap and attempted murder. He could have done well in life, but he ended up just another casualty in the War on Drugs.

Without Richard there to give me an excuse to use, I stayed stable for a while, and just smoked dope. I was on four milligrams of Bupe, the lowest maintenance dose I had ever started on after a fuck-up. This made me start to believe I had a chance to finally get clean. Even after all the failures in the past, I still wanted – needed – to try. But this time, I had to come out the other side a different person.

THE FINAL DETOX (2007)

I didn't rush anything this time. I was getting older, a little bit wiser, and I knew the way out had to come soon or I'd just be stuck in the rut of attempted recovery. I stayed on the Bupe for close to another year. I rarely used during this time, and I stopped travelling to Melbourne to see Carolyn. It was the best I'd done in twelve years, since I'd started using smack in the mid-90s.

My last detox was in September of '07. I went in determined to get free. A change in thinking had finally come over me. I wanted to stay clean more than I wanted to have 'just one more taste'. I felt like a fool for allowing myself to act the way I had for so many years. I'd hurt the ones who loved me the most, and I'd likely done irreversible damage to my body and mind while I pumped myself full of drugs for so long.

I needed to break free.

The changes in lifestyle I needed to make became much more important to me that any continuing drug use could ever hope to be. In August, I made the decision that the time was right.

Three weeks later I was back in The Bridge for detox, this time – finally – with the right headspace. I came off the low dose of Bupe and haven't looked back since.

I went in with the strongest desire I'd ever had to make it through. I didn't have a Carolyn or a Fee or an Amba waiting outside for me. I only had myself this time. And for the first time ever, I actually began to think that was all I needed.

I can't really say why this time was different. Why, after all the attempts, did I even bother? Maybe I'd finally worked out that it was almost past the point of no return.

The image of me as an old man shooting up flashed through my brain whenever I thought about getting on. I began to feel sick when I thought of injecting anything at all.

I still remembered a place of scrawled graffiti and scattered rubbish, of piss-soaked legs sticking out of a cubicle and water balloons blatant in a puddle of vomit. I remember lying in the park afterwards and wondering just what the fuck I was doing.

I knew some things, finally.

There is no way I can keep this up if I want to live. I can't use casually.

I can't use now and then.

I can't use at all.

I'm an addict and I'll always be one, no matter how long I stay clean.

There's no in-between, at least not for me. I have to never use again.

I didn't manage it straight away, but I did manage it.

The day I was released from detox, I had to walk down Victoria Street, past all the junkies and dealers I knew so well. This was when I always fucked up. When everything was right there in front of me. When it was easier just to say yes.

It was a gauntlet I needed to run. I didn't actually need to show myself I could do it. I knew I could. So I did it.

It felt cathartic to walk past all my former peers and the suppliers I knew so well, shaking my head to their offer of heroin, even though I had a bank account with a fresh social-security payment sitting there, just a withdrawal away from going back down that same old road I'd always driven. But not this time.

FREE

When I first wrote *Hammered*, I'd been free of all opiates for four years. At the time of this rewrite in 2019, it's been twelve.

In the early days, not long after getting out, I thought a hell of a lot about using. I thought about it nearly every day, and some nights I dreamt about it. When I first wrote this, four years later, it rarely (if ever) crossed my mind. In 2019, it's like it all happened to another person. I can't even imagine buying drugs and injecting myself. These days it only makes me feel queasy.

I do think it's something that will always be with me. I will remain an addict for the rest of my life. If I was stupid enough to shoot up heroin ever again, and continued to make that stupid decision every day, it would take no more than a week or two to regain my old addiction. I can never use heroin again. I don't want to use again. I now have too much to live for. I continued to smoke pot up until 2010, but even that was gone for a year now from the writing and now nine years since I've smoked anything apart from tobacco.

I've finally learnt to be happy in my own skin, a seemingly impossible task for most of my life.

I can now see a way to turn all the bad years around; to make them more positive. I can take that experience in the world of substance abuse and turn it into a way of helping people through their own journey. If I can do that, then none of it was a waste.

Lots of regrets follow me through the years, but I am who I am, the person who is sitting in a house we own writing this, because of what I have been through.

Since I made it through the other side, I have been searching for a release from the guilt and the disgust I still felt over all the wasted years. I've always been a voracious reader and writer, so the book you hold is my release.

It hasn't been easy to write, but in the end, I feel it was worth it.

It has helped me more than I can ever say to write this in 2011 and then rewrite it eight years later.

EPILOGUE

I ended up going back to tertiary study in Bendigo. I wanted to get some qualifications and become a drug counsellor. I still remembered just how important to my recovery the people at The Bridge were, and I wanted to give back to others the help I'd received through all those times in detox.

I had always been bright, and learnt without effort, and as a result had no trouble doing well in school. It was the same this time, too, and I managed to get a load of distinctions and high distinctions in the first year of the two-year Diploma of Community Welfare Work I chose to enrol in.

Then, at the end of the first year of my course, there came the time for placement, a six-week portion of study mid-diploma that involved working and studying in a real-world welfare facility that matched each student's field of interest. I tried to get that part of my course in the same community health clinic that had helped treat me in Echuca. I applied there, but the hospital board that oversaw the clinic denied the application, due to my criminal history. Because I was an ex-druggie with theft, piracy (film piracy, not that of the high seas) and drugs charges, I obviously couldn't be allowed into a community health centre and help people wanting to get off drugs.

With the guidance of the course co-ordinator, I applied at a few other drug & alcohol counselling facilities around the region, but none of them would take me either.

I ended up not moving on to the second year of that counselling course due to the placement issue. I managed to come up with another way to help people understand addiction. I decided to write my memoir, and started this manuscript.

It was around this time my mother became more and more ill, so I became a full-time carer for her in 2009.

In May 2009, my life's direction changed again when I met my future wife.

She is a beautiful woman, more than I ever thought I deserved but I guess I was wrong, and she supported me through the stages of writing this memoir. She has three wonderful kids who look up to me as both a role-model and a parent. Who could ask for more, considering my history? They all love me unconditionally, and their love is strong. Dawn has never used a drug in her life, but she understands me better and loves me more than anyone I have ever known.

Around Christmas of 2010, Mum was placed into respite over the holiday period, and place for full-time care in the nursing home in Rochester became available not long after, and she was happy there. She could see I was changing, and becoming the person she'd always known I could be. Her happiness with that was a great source of pride for me. I just wish Dad could have seen it before he passed.

The course psychology instructor at the college, Dr Ian Irvine, was a published writer, so he also taught in the same TAFE's writing and editing course. Late 2010, I applied for a position in that, and started studying full-time in 2011 to be a writer. After finding the online reading and writing community a few years back, I'd started sending out pieces of work to various publishers, and I'd had a run of luck with acceptances, so I was a published writer at this point, anyway. I went on to complete both years of a Diploma in Writing & Editing. After the first year, Dawn and I opened up Cohesion Editing & Proofreading, offering editing and layout services for writers and companies. Another year after that, in 2012, I finished my diploma and we started Cohesion Press, a small-press publisher of action-focused horror. If it had monsters, soldiers, and guns, we'd publish it.

I achieved many credit and distinction grades throughout my study, and when Dr Irvine pushed me to apply for recognition, the TAFE college rewarded my earlier struggles, combined with my later successes in education and the industry, with two awards at the graduation ceremony. I was awarded 2012 Vocational Student of the Year, as well as the major award of 2012 Student of the Year to recognise my industry success as a writer and publisher after overcoming my addiction and my many mistakes in life.

These awards were a definite highpoint of my recovery journey.

During this time, I'd also joined the Australian Horror Writers Association (AHWA) as a way to network with other creative types, and through a series of 'right place, right time' events, became the vice-president when the committee stepped down at an annual general meeting I attended. A year later, I stepped up even further to become president, which I held for two more years. During this time in the AHWA, I was the person who came up with the concept of writers' retreats in haunted locales as a fundraiser for the association and as a benefit to the members. It seemed natural to me after seeing the American Horror Writers' Association arranging similar events, a heap of horror writers in some haunted building for a weekend, getting inspiration for their art.

Dawn and I organised two of these events, both successful, and both held in decommissioned 1800s mental health hospitals in regional Victoria (both privately owned since being closed to patients in the mid-1990s). All attendees had great fun, spending the four days writing and the three nights hunting ghosts. Some lifetime friendships were born at these most unlikely of venues.

It was a hectic time at this point. I was studying online for a BA in Writing & Publishing as well as running Cohesion Editing and Cohesion Press with Dawn, who already had a BA in English Literature, and went back to study the same Diploma in Writing & Editing that I held.

We sure were kept pretty busy.

Then, in 2013, the editing teacher at TAFE was retiring, and he told the course co-ordinator the only person he trusted to teach editing within the requirements of the course was me. I was asked to go through the application process, and afterwards I was granted the position as teacher of editing for both levels of the course, first year and second year. I started when school went back in 2014, and worked part-time teaching the skills I'd only qualified in myself two years earlier. At the same time, I also ran the two businesses and studied online full-time to work at my BA.

Cohesion Press was going from strength to strength, and after a few initial releases, our very first SNAFU anthology was released in 2014, the same year I began teaching. My many contacts within the industry, from the early message-board contacts combined with people met through the AHWA presidency, ensured we included some New York Times-bestselling authors in the table of contents. This was the work we'd wanted to put out since the day Cohesion Press was first imagined. This was the success we'd hoped for, with the first SNAFU recouping its costs within twelve months, and following SNAFUs making their costs back even more quickly. We now have eight SNAFUs released in the wilds of online book retailers, and within them we've published some of the biggest names in the horror genre. We get fantastic sales and top Amazon rankings whenever we release a new edition, and for a while there had that nearly-impossible deal with a major US book distributor to have our print books pushed into every bookseller in North America.

That series of military horror stories also had one other unpredicted side effect a few years later.

In 2016 Hollywood came calling.

As a direct result of releasing SNAFUs worldwide, I can now say I've worked with a Hollywood superstar film-maker and director.

Tim Miller, the gentleman behind *Deadpool, Terminator: Dark Fate,* and Netflix's new series *Love, Death + Robots,* got in touch with me purely because he'd been a fan of SNAFU since the release of the first anthology. Tim loved short stories more than any other writing form, and he loved action-based speculative fiction (horror, sci-fi and fantasy), so our releases were like a dream come true for him. He wanted me to work for him on a project, helping pick stories from a large list and narrowing down what he had to read himself. He told me he rarely comes across someone with such similar taste in stories as himself.

He's now read every SNAFU we've released, and is writing the introduction for the next SNAFU anthology at the end of 2019.

💉 💉 💉

A year before Hollywood, in late 2015 and a few years since I'd stepped down from my role as a committee officer for the AHWA, something wondrous had come about as a result of my time there.

The private owner of one of the asylum facilities phoned me one Friday morning, out of the blue. We'd dealt with him when leasing space for our retreat at Beechworth Asylum in northern Victoria. He must have been impressed with Dawn and me for some reason or other, as he was calling to offer us a chance to buy a large portion of the asylum his company owned, and the purchase came with the exclusive rights to run ghost tours through the old asylum. A tour company had already existed in the facility for eight years, leasing the buildings for the tours, but the owner wanted them gone, as they were a leftover access-agreement from the previous owner, La Trobe University, and the current owner didn't get along with them at all.

The offer included vendor finance, so we could pay off the purchase price directly to the current owners. This gave us the option to say yes (we certainly didn't have the credit rating or the savings to get a loan so easily from a bank or building society) so after a few days' of doing figures and talking about how great an opportunity it could be, we accepted.

A large part of the decision came about from looking over income figures from the previous tour company. Also, Beechworth was in the centre of a major tourism region, and according to studies undertaken by local council, around half-a-million tourists visited the area every year. Many of these people went on ghost tours, and what was called 'Dark Tourism' was on the rise in the industry, and had been for a few years. We worked out we could definitely afford to run the tours and live frugally on the income from the tours, so we pushed ahead and moved from Bendigo to Beechworth at the end of 2015.

It was a massive risk.

If we didn't make enough income to cover the purchase agreement and our own basic rent, food and other expenses, we could have lost everything. I'd already left my role as a teacher, and all we could hope to fall back on was the free-lance editing work I could round up and the income from Cohesion Press. The way we both saw it, without risk, there would be little reward. And the risk was educated, based on the other group's figures and the costings outlined in all our enquiries before accepting and signing the purchase contract. All we had to lose was everything.

Our first tour was December of that year, and we've continued to grow since we opened Asylum Ghost Tours. We're slowly paying off the asylum buildings, and the titles will transfer to us soon. All up, we have around twelve-thousand square metres of asylum buildings, including the most historic and most haunted sections.

After eighteen months of trading, our company bought

another property, a modern three-bedroom house in Beechworth where Dawn and I now live. That purchase set us back a fair bit, but now, nearly two years after the purchase, the company has recovered and we're doing fine. The two years in between, well, we got through that, although the stress levels are only now receding. We're once again stable, and feeling like we're doing okay once more.

My journey has been a strange one indeed.

From being adopted from some orphanage in Carlton at three months old, to being abused ten years later by a predatory teacher, to being a speed freak hippie and hopeless junkie, and then on to teaching, then owner of multiple businesses and entrepreneur (and a nurse in between, just for something different).

I'm one of the lucky ones. These days, I have the love of a family and good friends I care for, and who care about me. Together we've built two successful businesses, bought property, and now we employ eight people.

Mum was still here when I first published *Hammered*, and she was happy that I'd finally grown up and settled down. Dad never got a chance to see me make it through the other side. I think he knew that one day I'd make it, but I can never be sure. I wish I could. It'd make life so much easier to know he still held the faith. It's too much to ask for, I guess, because even I didn't know if I'd make it. Not for most of my life. For some of it, I didn't want to.

It's a beautiful, sunny day.

Sitting here in front of the laptop, my back is sore and my hips hurt, which is becoming more common as the days go by, but the pain is a welcome friend. I've spent so many years throughout my life feeling nothing that the physical pain is a way of knowing that I'm truly alive... for the first time.

Geoff Brown August 2011/Rewrite February 2019

ABOUT THE AUTHOR

Geoff Brown was raised in Melbourne's gritty western suburbs by loving parents. He writes fiction, and is the author of many published short stories, newspaper and magazine articles, and his memoir. Longer works are forthcoming, but he can only write so fast.

With his wife Dawn, he is co-owner and co-director of Cohesion Press as well as tourism company Asylum Ghost Tours in Beechworth.

Shaun was a well-known face around Richmond. He was a long-term substance abuser who one day managed to contract a blood infection that damaged his spine and took away his ability to walk without some sort of aid. He ended up dying of a heart attack in his 40s.